CW00943840

japan
AT THE CUTTING EDGE

Hiroshi Hara Group, Sapporo Dome, Aerial View Perspective

COVER: Nikken Sekkei Ltd, Osaka Dome

Lighting Plan

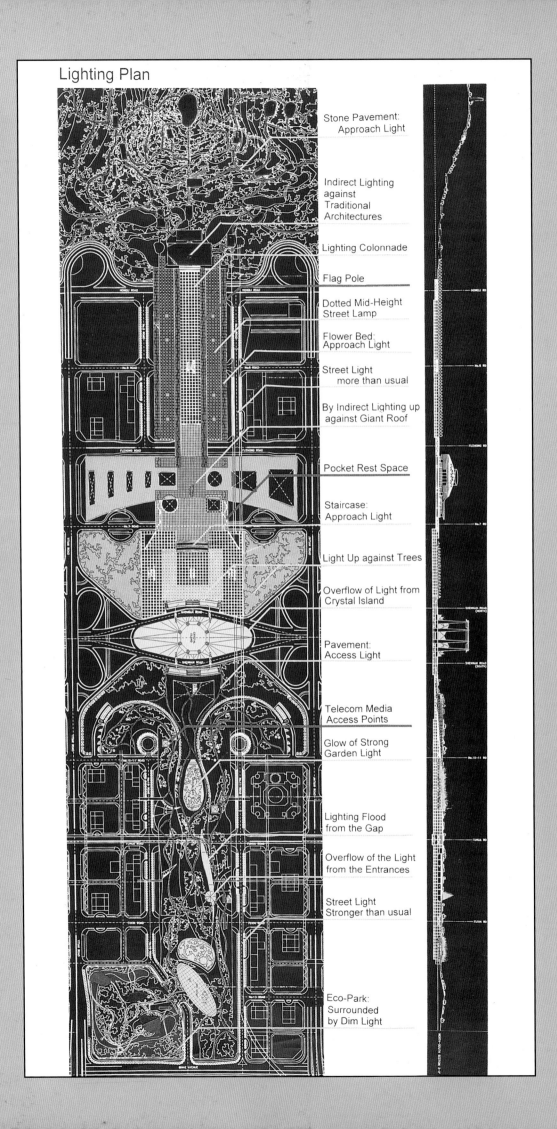

Stone Pavement:
Approach Light

Indirect Lighting
against
Traditional
Architectures

Lighting Colonnade

Flag Pole

Dotted Mid-Height
Street Lamp

Flower Bed:
Approach Light

Street Light
more than usual

By Indirect Lighting up
against Giant Roof

Pocket Rest Space

Staircase:
Approach Light

Light Up against Trees

Overflow of Light from
Crystal Island

Pavement:
Access Light

Telecom Media
Access Points

Glow of Strong
Garden Light

Lighting Flood
from the Gap

Overflow of the Light
from the Entrances

Street Light
Stronger than usual

Eco-Park:
Surrounded
by Dim Light

NEW**ARCHITECTURE**

japan

AT THE CUTTING EDGE

Shin Takamatsu + Shin Takamatsu Architect & Associates, Minatosakai Community Centre, Tottori Prefecture

OPPOSITE: Kisho Kurokawa, Shenzhen City, Republic of China

ANDREAS **PAPADAKIS** PUBLISHER

NEW ARCHITECTURE
1999 Number 3

Head Office
107 Park Street
London W1Y 3FB
United Kingdom

UK Tel.   0171 499 0444
UK Fax   0171 499 0222
Int. Tel.   +44 171 499 0444
Int. Fax   +44 171 499 0222
ISDN   +44 171 408 1317

Editor-in-Chief
Andreas Papadakis

Guest Editor: Botond Bognar
Senior Designer: Aldo Sampieri
Editors: Tom Dyckhoff, Vicky Braouzou
Assistant: Alex Papadakis

NEW ARCHITECTURE is available by subscription and in bookshops worldwide. Subscription rates for six numbers (including p&p) are £90.00/US$135. Individual issues are available at £17.50/US$27.50

Printed and bound in Singapore

Editorial Board:
Tadao Ando
Mario Botta
Peter Eisenman
Dimitri Fatouros
Kenneth Frampton
Meinhard von Gerkan
Jorge Glusberg
Michael Graves
Allan Greenberg
Hans Hollein
Josef Paul Kleihues
Panos Koulermos
Léon Krier
Kisho Kurokawa
Henning Larsen
Daniel Libeskind
Richard Meier
Enric Miralles
Jean Nouvel
Cesar Pelli
Demetri Porphyrios
Paolo Portoghesi
Peter Pran
Hani Rashid
Jacquelin Robertson
Alvaro Siza
Robert A.M. Stern
Bernard Tschumi

NEW ARCHITECTURE is an international journal of contemporary thought and practice in architecture and urban design. Designed with flair, it is edited and produced by a talented, experienced team that has excellent relations not only with the profession, academics and the schools but also with thinkers and world leaders who shape the society in which we live.

NEW ARCHITECTURE features survey and critical articles and presents the work and writings not only of all the top international architects but also of the young and innovative who have not yet made their mark. It looks critically at current directions, irrespective of stylistic and theoretical considerations, and explores each issue in depth raising all the important questions posed by the developing role of architecture in the world today.

NEW ARCHITECTURE carries up-to-date information and critical comment, and offers a platform for discussion on what is happening now in the worlds of Architectural Theory and Design, Urbanism, Design, Design Technology, Landscape, Interior Design, and the Fine Arts; it has features on significant competitions, exhibitions, conferences and books, and a special section devoted to the schools.

contents

Toyo Ito

Tadao Ando

THEORY AND DESIGN

Botond Bognar
Japanese Architecture:
Towards the twenty-first century
(A Report from the Site)   8

Toyo Ito
Three Transparencies   12

Masaharu Takasaki
Kagoshima Cosmology —
Reflections on the phantom of architecture   16

Kisho Kurokawa
Eco-media City   18

Tadao Ando
Beyond Minimalism   22

Gunter Nitschke
Urban Deity Grove   24

Evelyn Schulz
A Confucian Critique of Modern Tokyo
andits Future: Koda Rohan's
One Nation's Capital   28

FEATURED PROJECTS

Toyo Ito
Odate Jukai Dome   32

Hiroshi Hara Group
Sapporo Dome   40

Fumihiko Maki
Makuhari Messe   48

Tadao Ando
Garden of Fine Arts, Kyoto   54

Shin Takamatsu
Recent projects   60

An issue of this complexity would not have been possible without the wholehearted support of the thirty architects we had the privilege and pleasure of meeting during our visit to Japan. We should like to thank all of them for their time and hospitality. We are especially grateful to Kisho Kurokawa for the valuable discussions we had and for giving us the opportunity to view several of his buildings and preview his exhibition.

Special thanks to Tadao Ando as well as his associates, family and staff (especially Kulapat Yantrasast who acted as our guide) for their kindness in organizing extensive tours of their recent projects.

We should also like to thank: Hiroshi Hara for his eager response; Hiromii Fujii, Itsuko Hasegawa, Kunihiko Hayakawa, Arata Isozaki, Toyo Ito, Fumihiko Maki, Minoru Takeyama and Riken Yamamoto for showing us around their offices; Yasumitsu Matsunaga for organizing a useful meeting with Hajime Yatsuka and Ryoji Suzuki; Koji Yagi for his hospitality; Sentaro Hori, Eiichi Muramatsu and Tohru Ozasz from the Takenaka Corporation and Yutaka Kamiya and Hitoshi Kamura from the Shimizu Corporation for presenting their projects; Arakawa and Madeline Gins for showing us around their exhibition; Keiji Nakamura from the Intercommunication Centre for his helpful guidance on exhibitions at the Centre;

Oda, Curator of the Hiroshima City Museum of Contemporary Art; Syosuke Miyake from Theater Arts 1200, Kyoto, for showing us around the theatre. We are above all grateful to our guide in Japan, Professor Botond Bognar, and would like to thank him for his painstaking organization of our schedule to ensure that we became acquainted with the maximum number of architects and their work, for his company and advice, and for imparting to us his extensive knowledge of Japan, its culture, its people and especially its architecture.

0

Inside cover: Makoto Sei Watanabe; 3 Toshiyuki Kobayashi; 6-7 Botond Bognar; 9-11 Botond Bognar; 12-13 Alex Papadakis; 22 top left Mitsuo Matsuoka; Top right Tadao Ando; Bottom Shigeo Ogawa; 32-39 Mikio Kamaya; 56, 58 and 59 Shigeo Ogawa; 60-65 Toshiyuki Kobayashi; 66-71 Takeshi Taira; 72-75 Fujitsuka; 76-79 Botond Bognar; 80-85 Botond Bognar; 86-91 Katsuaki Furudate; 92-101 Tomio Ohashi; 102-107 Makoto Sei Watanabe.

© 1999 New Architecture Group Limited
All rights reserved. No part of this publication may be reproduced or transmitted in any form or by any means, electronic or mechanical, including photocopying, recording or any information storage or retrieval system without the written permission of the Publisher. Copyright of articles and illustrations may belong to individual writers, artists or architects. Neither the Editor nor New Architecture Group Limited hold themselves responsible for the opinions expressed by the writers of articles or letters included in this publication.

Itsuko Hasegawa and Andreas Papadakis at her studio

Botond Bognar and Hiroshi Hara

Hiromi Fujii
Folly in Matto City and
Passage in the Park   66

Riken Yamamoto
Iwadeyama Junior High School   72

Masaharu Takasaki
Kihoku Astrological Museum   76

Yoshio Taniguchi
Toyota Municipal Museum of Art   80

Arata Isozaki
Nagi Art Gallery   86

URBAN DESIGN

Kisho Kurokawa
Shenzhen City, China   92

LANDSCAPE DESIGN

M.S. Watanabe
Fibre Wave, K Museum   102

TECHNOLOGY

Nikken Sekkei Ltd.
Osaka Dome   108

THE SCHOOLS
Tokyo Institute of Technology
Shibaura Institute of Technology
University of Tokyo   122

COSMORAMA   128

INDEX   136

NEW BOOKS   137

Makoto-Sei Watanabe, K Museum with Fibre Wave on the left

Botond Bognar

Japanese Architecture:
Towards the twenty-first Century (A Report from the Site)

"This is without doubt a difficult time for...architects. However, life up to now may have been too carefree; like the grasshopper in the fable who whiled away time, it is necessary now to face up to the consequences. I am hoping that there will be an increase in architectural works or projects of a critical nature. The bubble era was full of events, but it produced few things of substance. Today is a time that calls for real content."

Riichi Miyake [1]

The "Bubble" and Beyond

The period between 1980 and 1992 was the era of Japan's "bubble economy" which, artificially inflated by land speculation, assured almost unlimited investment in architectural and urban development. Although much of the feverish construction during this period resulted, unavoidably, in frivolous and poor designs, it also yielded a vast number of outstanding, world-class projects, so much so that these years are often called the "new golden age of Japanese architecture." Think of such masterpieces as Fumihiko Maki's sports centres, Tadao Ando's many religious, educational, and commercial buildings or Kisho Kurokawa and Toyo Ito's numerous projects. Yet think also of the projects of a younger, equally diverse, generation of architects fostered through this period, such as Shin Takamatsu, Yoshio Taniguchi, Kazuyo Sejima, Ryoji Suzuki, Riken Yamamoto and Masaharu Takasaki. The fast paced development of Japanese cities provided plenty of work for both new and old architects. Japanese architecture and urban culture entered the information age, one of intensive globalization, a "new urban renaissance."

However, in 1992 the "bubble" burst and with it the favourable conditions for architecture. Japan is still struggling with its longest and most severe economic recession, with the end not quite in sight. Investment in construction, especially in the large-scale private sector, has diminished significantly, and even public investment, the usual remedy in economic slumps, cannot bolster the economy. The country's mood is understandably sombre, and among architects and construction firms, especially small ones, extremely pessimistic.

Yet, while construction has declined, it has not stopped entirely. In fact, if you were to visit Japan, unaware of its economic problems, you might think the country was booming, with city skylines crowded with cranes and building projects in full swing. This has much to do with the culture of building in Japan. Construction makes up a far greater proportion of Japan's GDP, around 20 per cent, than that of other developed countries.[2] Buildings are continually replaced. In Tokyo last year, for example, the well known Marunouchi Building, built in 1923 as one of Japan's first large urban complexes, was replaced by another large, but high-rise structure, now under construction.[3] So while it is being transformed at a slower pace, Tokyo is still living up to its reputation as an "ephemeral city."[4]

New Social Needs, New Public Architecture

So what drives Japanese architecture in this post-bubble era? One of the many positive outcomes of the "new golden age" of Japanese architecture is a heightened public awareness of architecture and its impact on the environment. Although architecture's popularization is a double-edged sword[5], it has at least prompted a demand for higher quality, well crafted architecture, new kinds of public facilities, and far better urban design. There is as a result a heightened awareness of the reciprocal relationship between architecture, urbanism and construction and the country's economic health. This has prompted the Government to foster new public projects. Although leaner times warrant a more prudent approach to design, quality still counts, even if it means building to solve discrete problems, rather than to create striking impressions. The excesses of the 1980s and early 1990s are now long gone. Instead the best legacies of "bubble economy" architecture are now directed to pressing social issues.

So, inevitably, most of today's construction – as many of the projects featured in this issue show – is for publicly financed buildings[6], to enhance the infrastructure of local communities, and ultimately the entire country, and to meet both current needs and those of the future. Such projects include schools, sports and leisure facilities, museums, community centres, port terminals, clinics and care centres for the elderly. The latter are increasingly important with Japan's rapidly aging population.[7] In fact there are several local and central governmental programmess to meet the urgent need for senior citizen facilities. Toyo Ito's Home for the Elderly in Yatsushiro (1994), Riken Yamamoto's Shimoizumi Care Plaza and Community Centre in Yokohama (1997), and Yamamoto Clinic in Okayama (1996) are all outstanding architectural examples of such new programmes. These impressive works reveal their designer's intention to provide not only adequate care for this growing segment of society, but also a better environment for an (inter)active community.

In turn new educational centres are also in demand to train all the workers in such public institutions; several are now under construction, including Yamamoto's Saitama Prefectural University of Nursing and Welfare in Koshigaya, near Tokyo, to be completed in 1999. New types of educational projects are also required to reinforce local communities. Many rural towns and villages, with reduced

birthrates and the emigration of the younger generation to larger cities, have had to consolidate their facilities while attracting local residents. Hiroshi Hara's Ose Secondary School in Uchiko (1992) and Yamamoto's spectacular Junior High School in Iwadeyama (1996), are in effect small "urban enclaves" which, besides working as schools, also serve as community centres.

Even sports centres and port terminals are built not only for their primary functions but also to support their communities in other, often incongruous ways, hosting exhibitions, shows, plays and concerts. The Odate Jukai Dome (note that most are not even called sports halls any more, but rather "domes") designed jointly by Toyo Ito and the Takenaka Corporation, and Minatosakai Ferry Terminal and Community Centre (1997), both designed by Shin Takamatsu, are cases in point. In so doing, they also draw in and establish connections to other regions and even other worlds. Masaharu Takasaki's astonishing design for the Kihoku Astronomical Observatory and Museum (1996), representing what he calls "an architecture of cosmology," is as much linked to outer space and cosmic regions as it is rooted in the special local character of Kagoshima where it is located.[8]

Ecology, Environment and Place

The diminished resources of the post-"bubble" economy have prompted a greater sensitivity among the public, Government and designers alike, to the protection of the environment and to the character of the site. Projects are increasingly shaped with their natural or urban "context" in mind. Context here is in inverted commas because the notion of context in Japan is more elusive than in other cultures, owing to the more ephemeral qualities of the Japanese environment, particularly the built one, and the Japanese sensibility to change.

Yet even large urban complexes are now more attuned to their environment than ever before. Kurokawa has designed a remarkable large-scale urban project for Shenzhen, a city north of Hong Kong, in which every part is designed to minimize harmful effects on the environment. The extensive underground parking, for example, is topped with a roof whose structural material and vegetation almost completely filters and absorbs exhaust fumes. Nikken Sekkei, Japan's largest design firm, has also been consistently involved in producing energy-conscious designs. Its Research Institute of Innovative Technology for the Earth (RITE), in Kyoto Prefecture (1993), was built to develop technology which protects the environment. Its own building is a perfect example, filled with energy saving and environment-protecting features, including solar energy and a new water cooling system, which reduces energy consumption by an additional 20 per cent. Reducing the harmful effects of wind power and insolation has also resulted in often bold and attractive design solutions. The large, bent wall in Yamamoto's Iwadeyama School is not only a protective screen against prevailing strong winds, but also a "spatial" device, which engenders a special mood or a sense of locality between sections of the building.

The best buildings not only solve ecological problems but also enhance human experience by forming memorable places. This is possible in both large and small projects, although perhaps the most exceptional results come from the tiniest places. Tadao Ando has long been acknowledged as one of the most gifted Japanese architects, whose works can transcend the confines of material reality to reach the highest levels of spirituality. His latest designs prove that this gift has not diminished. His tiny Meditation Space (1995), within the compound of the Paris UNESCO Headquarters, and the larger Garden of Fine Arts in Kyoto (1994) are masterpieces of architectural choreography and spatial sequencing. On one hand, they seem hardly more than attractively intricate outdoor promenades; on the other, they are far more than the sum of their parts. With the sparkle of cascading water, the contrast of light and shadow, the brush of a passing breeze, the whispering echoes of slow-moving footsteps, all within a profound silence, they are sites of spiritual journey. Ando's projects do not merely respond to, or respect their surroundings, but, more importantly, they transform them into what might be called, in Gaston Bachelard's words, "the poetics of space."[9]

This approach imbues works from an increasing number of other architects. Although Masaharu Takasaki, Yoshio Taniguchi and Ryoji Suzuki define place in different ways, through works as astonishing as the Kihoku Astronomical Observatory and Museum (1996), the Toyota Municipal Museum of Art (1996), and the Sagishima Ring (1995), all are both inspired by and make and important contribution to their unique and spectacular settings.

New Technology, New Landscape

The increased attention to the environment is also revealed in the growing number of successful landscape design projects. Landscaping was once not as well developed as architecture; more often than not buildings were constructed in utilitarian surroundings of driveways and parking lots. Green areas or gardens were rare, and even then relegated to leftover pieces of land. This is, of course, something of a paradox, since traditional Japanese architecture has been long cherished as an integral part of nature, the carefully designed "artificial" landscape. In modern Japan, however, this "artificial"

landscape has rarely been cultivated to the standard of old. Today the situation is rather different. Not only have the Japanese rediscovered the need for a new symbiotic relationship between architecture and landscape, but they have also focused attention on a new generation of landscape designers.

There are many new models for, and innovative interpretations of "landscaping." Ando's Garden of Fine Arts, for instance, is a novel design, and, somewhat in the same vein, Taniguchi's Toyota Museum displays several features – the enclosed Japanese sculpture garden, the long canopy connecting the two wings, and the ramp leading to the lower plaza – that are as much part of the landscape as they are of the building. The success of Taniguchi's design relies largely on his collaboration with the renowned American landscape designer, Peter Walker. Walker, like several other foreign landscape designers, now finds himself as busy in Japan as at home; even large design firms, such as Nikken Sekkei, occasionally rely on his services, as in the case of Solid Square (1995), a twin tower office building in Kawasaki City, where landscaping mediates between inside and out.

Landscape and garden are part of architectural metaphor too. Inspired by the age of electronics and information, Toyo Ito has written about his recent works as "a garden of microchips;"[10] Hara's notion of an "electronic garden" reveals a similar preoccupation.[11] Itsuko Hasegawa, on the other hand, considers her architecture to be "second nature:"[12] "I use architectural and technological details to evoke nature, and natural and cosmic details to evoke architecture."[13] Likewise, in his Tower of Wind at Yokohama, Toyo Ito, as early as 1986, used computer technology and electronics to display natural phenomena. More recently Makoto-Sei Watanabe has employed solar cells and tiny light-emitting diodes on top of a forest of carbon fibre rods to illuminate the motion of wind as they sway against the evening sky. In effect, what we witness in these landscape designs as well as in many other projects, such as Nikken Sekkei's Hisaya Park in Nagoya (1989), is the merging of the notions and workings of (high) technology and nature.

New technologies shape architecture as well as landscape: look no further than the growing number of large domes.[14] The large spans of such projects as the Odate Jukai Dome (1997) by Toyo Ito and the Takenaka Corporation are conceived through bold tectonics and the application of innovative structural systems. But technology is also at work in the craftsmanship of many other designs. Taniguchi's works, including the Visitors' Centre at the Tokyo Sea Life Park (1996) and the Toyota Municipal Museum of Art (1996) are distinguished by their superb spatial qualities, exceptional detailing, and the innovative use of a wide range of materials, especially new types of glass, high strength metals, and stone.

Japanese architecture today seems to have entered a new era not merely because of the limitations of the post-bubble economy, but also because it is shaped by much broader considerations. This is a new modernism in architecture, which, like its predecessor, aims to respond to the times in which it is conceived, and to shape those of the future. Yet, unlike early modern architecture, the new modernism, while determined to avoid the pitfalls of both universalism and shallow postmodernism, is more sensitive to the particularities of its creation; it is more capable of coping with the heterogeneous, even contradictory, conditions of today's society and the urban conditions in which it is set.

The quality of substance that Miyake called for is now, more than before, an integral part of architectural production in Japan. In this sense, the renewed, reinterpreted, yet also much more flexible Japanese modernism not only responds to contemporary society, but also, as Miyake hoped, assumes a critical position within it.

PREVIOUS PAGE: Itsuko Hasegawa, Shonandai Cultural Centre, Fujisawa City
THIS PAGE:
TOP: Shibuya Station Square, Tokyo
MIDDLE: Toyo Ito, Home for the Elderly, Yatsushira
BOTTOM: Ryoji Suzuki, Sagishima "Ring" Guest House, Mihara
OPPOSITE: RoTo Architects (USA), Warehouse C, Nagasaki

1 Riichi Miyake, "The Age of Uncertainty" in *JA* (The Japan Architect), 1994-1 Annual, p.51.

2 *Japan: An Illustrated Encyclopedia*. Tokyo: Kodansha, 1993, p.235., and Japan Almanac 1997. Tokyo: Asahi Shimbunsha, 1996, p.159.

3 The eight-storey building was designed by the Mitsubishi Goshi Company, with the assistance of the Chicago-based Fuller company. With a total floor area of 60,000 sq.m, the Marunouchi Building was not only the largest structure at the time of its completion, but – with a complete line of shops and facilities, such as restaurants and auditoriums, on its first and second floors, and outfitted with the most advanced mechanical equipment – also the first really modern urban complex in Japan.

4 For further reading on the ephemerality of Japanese architecture and urbanism, see B. Bognar, "What Goes Up Must Come Down: Recent Urban Architecture in Japan" in *Durability and Ephemerality - Harvard Design Magazine # 2* (Fall 1997), pp.33-43.

5 In the 1980s and early 1990s, architects were often treated as popular icons or superstars, while their designs were regarded as highly fashionable commercials or commodities.

6 The past couple of years have witnessed the completion of many other large-scale projects as well, such as the Tokyo International Forum (1997) by the American architect Rafael Viñoly, and the New Kyoto Station Complex (1997) by Hiroshi Hara; yet these enormously expensive projects, designed and built over many years are still the products of "bubble" times.

7 The percentage of the elderly (over 65 years of age) in Japan was 14% in 1995, and is predicted to be 17% in 2000, 24% in 2015, and 26% in 2030. The birthrate (number of live births per woman) in 1995 reached 1.43, the lowest ever recorded, and the situation is not improving. The 2.1 births, necessary to maintain a steady number of population was last recorded in 1974. (All these data are quoted from *Japan: An Illustrated Encyclopedia*. Tokyo: Kodansha, 1993, and *Japan Almanac 1997*. Tokyo: Asahi Shimbunsha, 1996).

8 For further details see *Takasaki Masaharu: An Architecture of Cosmology*. New York: Princeton Architectural Press, 1998.

9 Gaston Bachelard. *The Poetics of Space*. Boston: Beacon Press, 1969.

10 Toyo Ito, "A Garden of Microchips: the Architectural Image of the Microelectronic Age" in *JA Library 2*, Tokyo: The Japan Architect, 1993 (Summer), p.4.

11 Hiroshi Hara is quoted in Günter Nitschke, "From Ambiguity to Transparency. Unperspective, perspective, and aperspective paradigm of space" in *Japan Today*. Louisiana Revy Vol.35, No.3, June 1995.

12 Itsuko Hasegawa, "Architecture as Another Nature – and Recent Projects" in *Aspects of Modern Architecture*, AD Architectural Design, London, 1991. p.14.

13 Itsuko Hasegawa, "3 Projects" *The Japan Architect*, Nov/Dec, 1986, p.55.

14 Many of these new multi-purpose sports facilities are constructed to meet the needs of such international sports events as the Nagano Winter Olympics in 1997 and the Soccer World Cup in 2002.

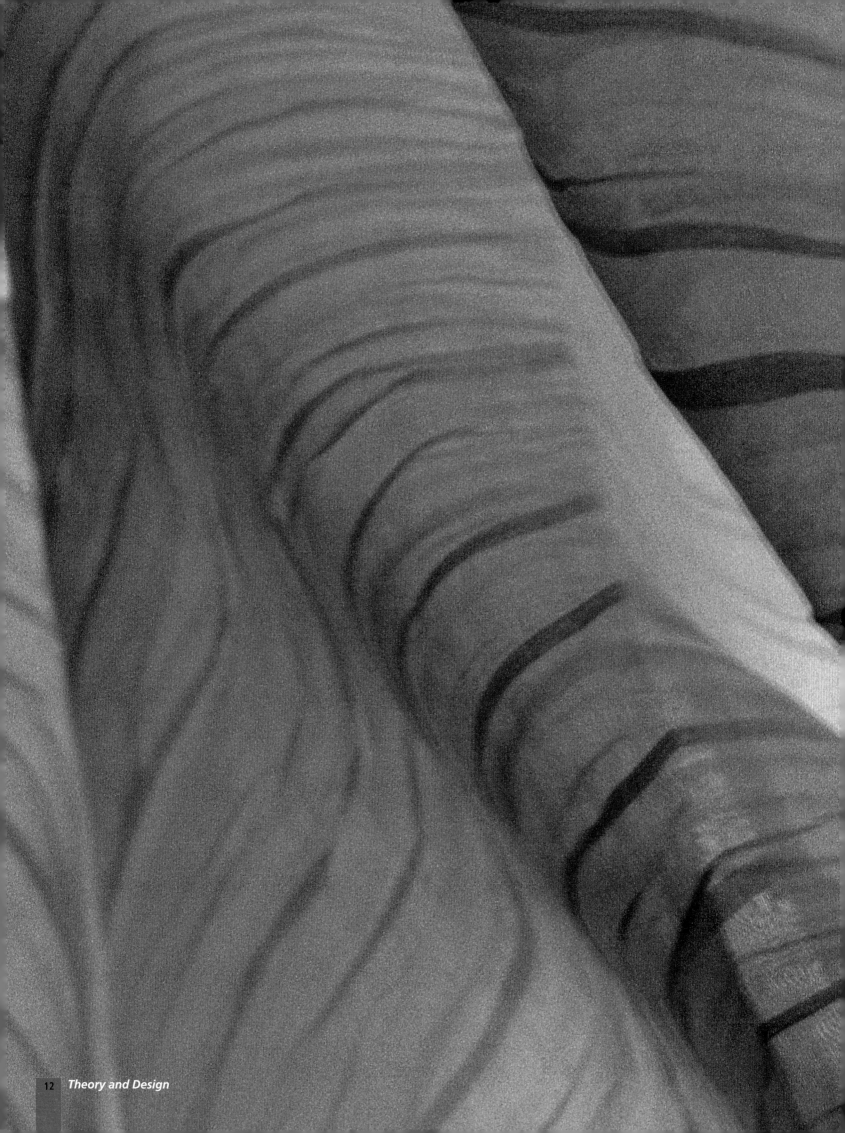

Toyo Ito

Three Transparencies

Fluid Transparency

To stand before a giant fish tank at the aquarium is to experience the curious sensation of being in two places at once. With only a clear wall in between, 'here' on this side one is on dry land surrounded by air, while 'over there' on the other opens an aquatic world. Not so long ago, aquarium tanks were relatively small affairs, peered at through windowlike openings in the wall. Today's aquariums, however, have impossibly huge tanks where awesome volumes of water press at us with awesome force through layers of acrylic tens of centimetres thick.

To see through walls like this represents a major paradigm shift, as different as architectural elevations and cross-sections. When looking through a window, the view beyond is inviolate, self-contained. Not so with a transparent wall; an environment that ought to permeate everywhere suddenly cuts off at an invisible boundary, leaving its sheared face fully exposed. A visit to the aquarium in days gone by was like going to the circus; now one is fully immersed in the experience.

Thanks to these new aquariums, we now have a clearer image of aquatic life: how the underwater plants and animals move in ways unimaginable above ground, particularly in deeper, previously inaccessible waters, where the increased water pressure makes the deep-sea swimmers lethargic, the swaying fronds heavy. Like the subdued dramatics of Noh theatre, all is continuous movement caught in a slow-motion time warp, each cell and body part suspended at half-speed. Moreover, the reduced transparency of water shows everything as if through a silk curtain. A gauzelike diffusion that sets the reality of things off at a fixed distance. One loses the vital physicality; we see glazed fruits floating in a gelatine universe.

In one project currently under construction, my initial image was of an aquatic scene. Sited in the very heart of the city, facing onto an avenue lined with large beautiful cedars, a transparent cubic volume rises seven storeys from a 50 metre by 50 metre square ground plan. Seven thin floor-layers are supported by thirteen tubelike structures, each irregular non-geometric tube resembling a tree root, thicker towards the top as it nears the soil surface, splaying and bending slightly. These hollow tubes are sheathed in a basketry of plaited steel piping, mostly covered in frosted glass. The effect is that of hollow translucent candles.

In the margin beside my first sketches for these tubes I wrote: Columns like seaweed. I had imagined soft tubes slowly swaying underwater, hose-like volumes filled with fluid. Without resorting to the typical wall-with windows – no glass facade dividing the building from the street, no clear acrylic plate out of a massive fish tank – I wanted to express the cut face to another world.

But why the aquatic image for a building on solid ground? For one thing, water is the primal shape-giver, the source to which all life forms trace back. Trees, for example, as they branch out recursively from trunk to twig to leaftip resemble nothing so much as rivers that gather tributary streams and empty into the sea. The thick opacity of the trunk dividing into ever-finer branches, gradually forming an intricate membrane, and finally attaining the near-transparency of the leaves – the very image of fluidity.

If this is true of a tree above ground, how much more fluid then those plants and animals that exist underwater? Their very forms embody such movement. As with fish fins, those parts that suggest movement grow more transparent further out towards the tips. Motion and form meet in fluidity, and fluidity is always translucent-to-transparent.

Erotic Transparency

Translucent objects always seem to be in transition from opaque to transparent. I am reminded of insect metamorphosis: the transparent larvae just out of their hard pupae are covered with a milky liquid; then in an instant, contact with air turns them into adult insects with hard, clear wings. A half-formed translucent gel state stirs transformative imaginings; the moment it turns transparent and solid and fixed, that ambiguous fascination is lost.

Certain architecture, such as the early works of Mies van der Rohe, almost attain such gelatinous, near-fluid transparency. Known as the creator of transparent glass-and-steel twentieth-century architecture, Mies at the beginning of his career built with opaque materials – brick and stone. Then suddenly in the 1920s, his architecture undergoes a metamorphosis. In sketches for 'Glass Skyscrapers' and his Barcelona Pavilion interior, fluid translucent spaces truly come to life.

The Barcelona Pavilion, the German pavilion at the 1921 Barcelona World's Fair, was steel in structure, but it was stone and glass that gave it flamboyant dynamism. The stone mosaic covering the abstract planar formation of the walls describes a boldly fluid wave pattern. Poised between these stone-faced walls, greenish frosted glass screens give the impression of tanks fitted with water. The various planes play across at right angles, but never actually intersect. Rather, they overlap with the shallow outdoor pool surfaces to create a fluid space: the very image of solid form slowly melting away to a liquid state. A most erotic space.

Similarly, the Japanese designer Shiro Kuramata was keenly attuned to such transparency in contemporary society, and actually pursued it in his creative work. Very intuitively, at times playing the 'villain' of bad taste. From the start of his career in the 1960s, he frequently used clear acrylic in his furniture designs.

In one such acrylic chair, the furniture-object virtually disappears, leaving only the 'primitive' act of sitting. His clean wardrobes and bureau-dressers were even more powerful in this regard. The reason being that storage, the act of putting things away, is essentially one of hiding objects in opaque, unseen places. But here, far from hiding them, the clothes on hangers and folded garments are displayed floating in space. The material box-forms vanish and only the act of storage remains – in an erotically charged space, might we add. The effect of his transparent touch was not unlike trespassing in some forbidden room, catching a glimpse of what one is not supposed to see.

Three years before his death, one particular Kuramata design made direct gesture to the eroticism of the transparent. The clear acrylic chair 'Miss Blanche' (1988) achieved a heightened transparency by scattering artificial roses through its 'empty' interior. The red petals float this way and that as if drifting in a stream; floral patterns released from the heavy upholstery fabrics of old and turned into real flowers suspended in clear, liquid space.

Where making things transparent seemingly ought to have been the most abstract of acts, a divesting of form into pure space, suddenly there appears an all-too-real, even seductive presence. This polarity, these startling reversals, this real-unreal ambiguity are distinctly transparent tastes.

Opaque Transparency

Transparency, however, is not always so light and clear. We Japanese have willingly surrendered any opacity of self so as to blend into today's society. We live see-through lives, undistinguished from anyone else in an extremely streamlined regulatory system. Urban Japan has become a convenience store peopled by instant snack foods wrapped in plastic and lined up on a shelf. We are mere signs, wholly transparent, devoid of any scale of value. What's more, this mediocre transparent existence is entirely comfortable. And yet, as the individual in contemporary society turns ever more transparent, architecture and the city are becoming conversely more opaque.

One major characteristic of the contemporary city is that each space is utterly cut off from the next. Interiors partitioned room from room, walls everywhere. Such perhaps is the destiny of social control: a vast homogenised cityscape is fragmented into places with almost no spatial interrelationships. This is especially true in commercial spaces, where divorcing the interior from the external environment facilitates dramatically 'staging' the premises. Spaces thick with shining product are clearly set up, when seen from a slight remove, on the basis of their uniformity and particularity; spaces seemingly so idiosyncratic are merely the accumulation of introspectively inflated fragments of homogeneity – this is today's city.

Walking through Shinjuku or Shibuya Station, two of the most complex spatial configurations in central Tokyo, is a very strange experience. All the criss-crossed levels of communication, intersecting train and subway lines, the three-dimensional knots of interlinking pedestrian passageways between, commercial spaces surrounding and interpenetrating and surmounting this maze, everything is designed to make us lose our way inside a viewless world almost entirely cut off from the outside. All we have to go on are signs and verbalised cues. While we are in the midst of this complicated spatial experience, it is all we can do to create a correspondingly abstract and semioticised mental space.

What is demanded of today's architect is to discover 'relationships' between such hermetic, fragmented spaces; to seek opaque-yet-transparent connections between multilayered spaces. In a project commissioned by one Japanese city, a Fire Department completed two years ago, I tried to realise an 'opaque transparency.' Almost all functional aspects of the building were raised on rows of columns to the upper storey. This so-called 'pilotis' structure allowed the ground floor to maintain a continuity with the street in the form of a parklike space left open and accessible to all. The only provision is that a dozen or more fire trucks and ambulances and various pieces of training equipment be kept there as well. In the middle of a turfed area, two tower structures large and small are strung with climbing ropes and a long rope bridge between for the fire brigade's daily exercises. There is also a drowning-rescue practice pool and a small gym. The townsfolk can drop by and watch the fire fighters go through their paces; meanwhile the corridors connecting the individual rooms on the upper storey look down onto whatever is going on below. There are even lightwells through the upper storey floor to allow communication between levels. All this is designed to give the fire brigade a 'face' in the daily life of the town, not just in the event of an emergency.

The building is not by any means glassed-in or transparent. However, openings here and there in the floor make for a certain dynamic between levels above and below – what I call 'opaque transparency.' Glass buildings aren't the only way to achieve transparency; no, the task on hand today is how to forge relations between otherwise walled-off spaces.

In *The Mathematics of the Ideal Villa and Other Essays* (MIT, Cambridge, 1976), Colin Rowe terms such relations 'phenomenal transparency' as opposed to 'literal transparency.' In the title essay he cites by way of 'phenomenal' examples the early works of Le Corbusier or the paintings of Ferdinand Léger; and 'literal,' the Bauhaus architecture of Walter Gropius and the artworks of Lazlo Moholy-Nagy. In other words, while the latter is merely composed of transparent elements, the former layers non-transparent 'blind' elements so as to create transparent interrelationships. Take, for instance, Le Corbusier's famous early work, the 'Villa Stein' at Garches (1927) and its abstract layering of overlapping vertical and horizontal planes. The effect is such that despite the actual volume of the physical building, the composition becomes a cubist painting with planes of no visual depth advancing and receding in non-Euclidian space.

Now more than ever, architecture must deliver such spatial relationships. For despite our apparent transparency, like all-too-colourless products lined up in a convenience store, we continue to build ever more solid barriers between us. Not that we should return to the world-without-walls collective existence of times past – even if we could. The key lies in introducing new openings through the walls we have already built.

Masaharu Takasaki, Kagoshima Cosmology, colour rendering

Masaharu Takasaki

Kagoshima Cosmology – Reflections on the phantom of architecture

In Kagoshima Prefecture, which lies at the most south-westerly tip of Japan, there is a volcanic mountain range which consists of Sakurajima, Kirishima and Kaimondake. Sakurajima, especially, which erupts even today, is a symbol of the dynamism of this land. In this particular environment there is also the East China Sea to the west, the Pacific Ocean to the south-east and south, and also many large and small islands that deserve attention. The imported cultures came with the flow of the Black Current – the southern character that has the power to stimulate even the hardened spirit of today's people. The ocean, as calm as a mirror of still water, keeps the awesome energy of the volcano deep underground. The peculiar land form relates with the energy of fire, soil and water, existing with pride and exuding an impression of indescribable spirituality.

Today Kagoshima is no more than a sacred place. One can imagine from such topographic characteristics that it is the absolute place with an abundance of affection for ancient times, without respect for its history, where the myths of the Deity come down. It is one of several places in the prefecture where the peculiar culture to which ancient shamanism belongs is still alive today.

Some may have the same feelings about the place through strange imaginings. In my case, I feel a great burst of energy when I sense the power of the land where the energy of fire, soil and water is rife. This feeling is like communicating with an inner world beyond visible communication, the sensitive communication of a consciousness of primeval human nature. It is a similar feeling to the moment when our consciousness is overcome or our soul stunned by the appearance of a sacred phantom. That momentary floating feeling is similar to the separation of the body from the soul. The land, longing for ancient times, like a topographic Mandala, intuitively penetrates the hard shell of modern civilization.

Why has such a configuration appeared here? There are many such places in Kagoshima that show their strong will to be there. I do not know any other place like this land which strengthens so much my yearning for its original topography. In Kagoshima, the ancient and the present coexist and there is a mystery in which the imagination comes unconsciously. It is the sacred illusion, drawn from reaction to the imagination, that goes beyond theory and technique. It is a provocation against super-modernism. The ancient energy, which flows through and all over the topographic Mandala always connects with a future of one thousand years later. The history of Kagoshima from primeval times is not yet complete; the energy in the volcano range has an inner rhythm of returning to the past and moving towards the future concurrently. It might have to react to the sacred rhythm of energy to create the utopia of Kagoshima Cosmology today. Kagoshima Cosmology, which emerges from consideration of a phantom, could coordinate the opposite vectors of the past and the future and would only become a present-day utopia in a place where its essence is found through the ages, both ancient and future.

I am searching for a kind of architecture that would be suitable for such a sacred place. In my first project in Kagoshima – Zero Cosmology – the zero form emanates from the phantom where ancient feeling and the future coexist, and the symbolic small cosmos of Kagoshima Cosmology is an actual utopia as if by revelation. In that universal egg, the zero as eternal life, deathless time runs along. All things come around with timeless essence and subconscious matters are accepted. I shall continue to cling to the floating feeling of architecture here in Kagoshima as if the architecture has come to fly from the future. A style giving an impression of floating is my idea for architecture in Kagoshima. The absolute land, which is calling out to ancient times, is wounded by our current blunt civilization and pays attention to the future while it considers ancient times. My architecture will continue to reject landing here, in the present. The architecture exists in the present but it is absent from this era and goes to other places or times. The presence of architecture stimulates the human sub-conscious. A mysterious world is created in the utopia in the subconscious. It is towards this fantasy that architecture should aim spiritually.

Sacred places invite holy architecture. To answer the invitation of the Deity, it is necessary to foretell the future situation one thousand years later. Architecture should land on earth as if it came from a distant universe. The appearance of architecture means not only anchored in the present but also anchored in history. The paradise of Kagoshima Cosmology has appeared vividly in the consciousness of space.

In the topographical Mandala of Kagoshima, there is much in nature that looks like the designed form of God. For instance, "The Standing God in the Office" of Amami Osima is a big rock standing in the sea and it is the "place of God," drawn in the Mandala. In addition, it is the place where the shaman might say, "Oh God, please be seated here." It would be the fantasy of architecture, the coincidence of existence and absence deeply connected with human consciousness. "Oh God, please be seated here" – the shaman's voice echoes in my timeless illusion. Kagoshima Cosmology is the true home of architecture.

Pedestrian Network

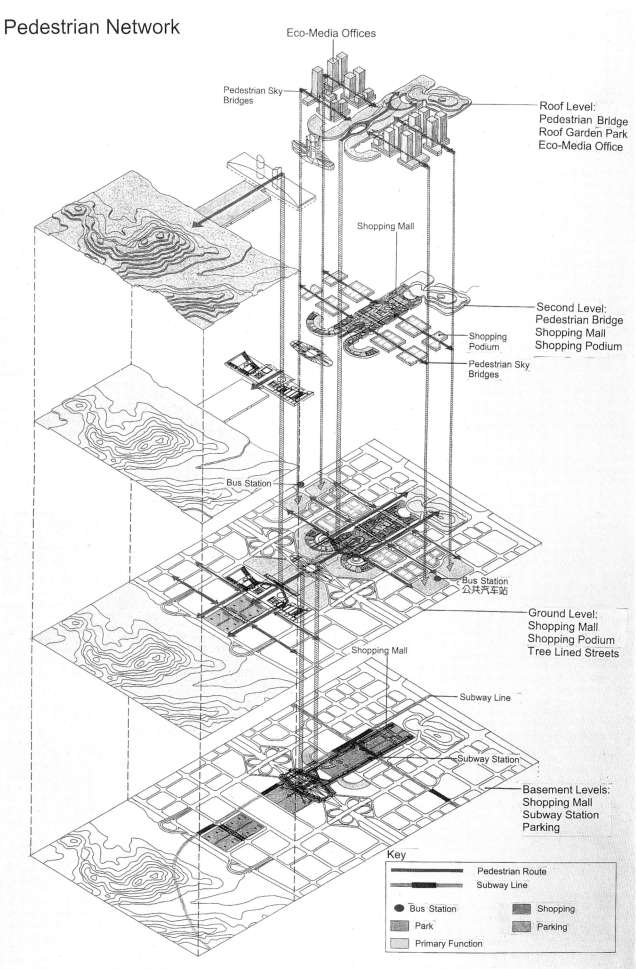

Eco-Media Offices

Pedestrian Sky Bridges

Roof Level:
Pedestrian Bridge
Roof Garden Park
Eco-Media Office

Shopping Mall

Second Level:
Pedestrian Bridge
Shopping Mall
Shopping Podium

Shopping Podium

Pedestrian Sky Bridges

Bus Station

Bus Station
公共汽车站

Ground Level:
Shopping Mall
Shopping Podium
Tree Lined Streets

Shopping Mall

Subway Line

Subway Station

Basement Levels:
Shopping Mall
Subway Station
Parking

Key

Pedestrian Route	
Subway Line	
● Bus Station	Shopping
Park	Parking
Primary Function	

The public space design of the central axis of Shenzen city centre; pedestrian network

Kisho Kurokawa

The Eco-Media City in the Age of Symbiosis

A great change is occurring all over the world. It is occurring in a chain reaction in all realms of human activity — politics, business technology, the arts, and culture — as well as in all areas of academic study and research, from biology, chemistry and quantum dynamics, to philosophy, architecture, and urban planning.

It is difficult to describe these changes in a word, but perhaps we can summarize them as a move towards an age of symbiosis, a paradigm shift from the era of the machine to the era of life. The idea of symbiosis is at the heart of Mahayan Buddhist thought, which has profoundly influenced Japanese culture from the fourth century. Recently, though, it has become detached from Buddhism and evolved into a new way of thought for all spheres of twenty-first century society, including politics, economics, the arts and culture, and science and technology. I call this new age the age of symbiosis. It is an age of the symbiosis of different cultures, of eastern and western cultures, of reason and emotion, of science and technology and art and culture, of tradition and innovative technology, the symbiosis of different generations, and of humanity and nature.

Asia still nurtures a lifestyle that considers architecture and man as a part of nature. The Asian lifestyle, which logocentrism regarded as unscientific and not modern, is now being re-evaluated because of the importance of deciphering nature sensitively, and feeling and learning the wisdom of nature with all our senses.

Around 1960 I created a word, or concept, "kyosei" (symbiosis). A year earlier I predicted that "we will see a paradigm shift from the era of the machine in the first half of the twentieth century towards the era of life in the early twenty-first century," and used the biological term "kyosei" (cohabitation). Then I looked to the Buddhist term "tomoiki" and changed the reading of the Chinese characters in order to create a new word "kyosei" (symbiosis).

The Japanese language has words such as harmony, adjustment, coexistence, unification and compromise, which cannot describe the concept (philosophy) of symbiosis. Therefore I created the word "kyosei" = symbiosis.

My definition of "kyosei" at the time was:

1. We oppose and compete with each other, yet we need each other.

2. We respect and do not intervene in each others' different religions and cultures while we actively try to expand common grounds and mutual understanding.

3. Together we can create things that cannot be created by oneself alone.

4. We exist by giving to and receiving from each other.

5. We are linked to each other by biological cycles.

Ten years later, in 1971, a prominent American economist, Mr.

Kenneth Boulding, visited Japan, and I had an opportunity to converse with him on a television programme. Mr. Boulding brought a global environmental viewpoint to economics and advocated ecosystems with ecology in mind. This was his famous concept of Spaceship Earth, in which he proposed that the earth needs to have ecosystems with a recycling system, just as a spaceship does. This discussion was the first time I used the word "eco-city" in correspondence with ecosystems in economics. Nowadays the concept of eco-city is used worldwide, together with the words "information society" and "symbiosis" that I created.

By definition the age of symbiosis originates from a critique of Euro-centrism, logo-centrism and rationalistic dualism, the conceptual underpinnings of modernism. Modernism held that humans, as possessors of reason, enjoyed a privileged status among all living things, and that this reason could reveal an ideal and ultimate truth. It placed greatest value on scientific technology and economic activity, judged by the criteria of reason, and affirmed objectively and scientifically.

In architecture and urban planning since the Renaissance this idealism drove the search for the ideal city and design. CIAM, for instance, in its Athens Declaration, defined a "universal theory", an international style of architecture and and modern city planning, as the one ideal truth in architecture, existing universally and transcending all cultural differences. The international style was an extremely convenient model for industrial society, based as it was on the factory system of mass production, just like televisions, automobiles and other industrial products.

In methodology, modernism was supported by rationalistic dualism, which explains all existence by dividing it into pairs of opposing elements: flesh and spirit, conservation and reform, interior and exterior, humanity and nature, the city and the country, science and art, the part and the whole, matter and spirit, East and West, and so forth. The intermediate, characterized by the ambiguity of the inchoate and the periphery, by multivalency, was rejected as unscientific.

This binomial opposition or dualism created a method in architecture and urban planning in which the building or the city was analyzed, divided into its different functions, and then recombined as a whole. Policies of zoning and land use based on the division of the city's parts by function were derived from this rationalistic dualism.

From the time of the Meiji Restoration in 1868, Japan has made a thoroughgoing effort to imbibe such Western culture and modernize itself. The concept that Westernization equals modernization and progress has been accepted as self-evident not only in Japan but in all developing nations, the ultimate aim being the transformation of all cultures around the world into one homogenized, dominant Western culture.

Yet there are now signs that this modernist world order is changing to one of symbiosis. First, the industrial age is transforming into the information or post-industrial age. This change is not revolutionary, in which all the achievements of the past are rejected. It is instead a double structure, in which the new information society grows on top of the previous industrial society. Whereas the industrial age was characterized by the mass production of homogeneous products, the average man (what Heidegger called Das Mann), and the homogeneous society, the information age, by contrast, is becoming one that creates information and images, and which values individuality and creativity, and the identity of regional culture.

It is the dawning of an era more rigorous than that of industry. A society that emphasizes individuality and creativity is naturally a diverse society. We are already seeing a shift from a time when control was exercised by large organizations and macro engineering to a time of bold opposition to large companies driven by small business and individuals backed by venture capital. Each person will awake to their individuality, and creativity. Each of the world's countries, large or small, will awake to its own ethnic or folk culture. There is a growing recognition that the world's many cultures are distinct and precious and that their survival in the future contributes to the richness of life on earth. It could well be an age of conflict both cultural and religious. Yet, advances in transportation and communication will spur an immediate transition to a borderless age. A closed society is already impossible. The only course of action is to strive for the symbiosis of different cultures through dialogue and solidarity as confrontation and competition continue. These different cultures must exist in relationships of mutual respect, education, as well as competition. Another way of describing this ideal is open regionalism. A concrete example of this symbiosis is the treaty on biological diversity signed three years ago in Brazil, drafted to protect species on the verge of extinction.

Second, there is a shift in economic development, as Rostow's linear development theory, characterized by economic stages, gives way to non-linear economic development. In 1960, the American economist Rostow proposed that every country passes through the same stages in economic development, taking off from early development through maturation to sophisticated mass consumption. Western Europe, the United States and Japan have obviously passed through these stages to reach the information age. The waves of the information age, however, now break on the shores of every country of the world regardless of their stage of economic development. Even people in developing countries can receive satellite television broadcasts or satellite telecommunications as long as they have a parabolic antenna. The Internet has linked the world's PCs in almost no time at all to form a global computer communication network with no distinction between developed and developing countries. Every day, more than 2,000 people access my home page, from both developed countries and developing countries, where they view my projects, read books, fill out questionnaires, and participate in discussions. We are standing on the threshold of a new era of economic symbiosis in which countries at all stages of economic development can support part of the global economic system while making maximum use of their own resources, industrial structure, climate, topography, and culture.

Third, there is a transformation from the age of Mediterranean culture to the age of Pacific — particularly Asian — culture, parallel with the change from the age of the principle of machines, to the age of the principle of life. Technology in the twentieth century was visible and mechanistic — steam engines, water and thermal power generation, electricity from atomic power, aircraft, and automobiles, and developed outward from the Mediterranean Sea. This era has reached the end of its course. In comparison, the twenty-first century will be a time of symbiosis between nature and electronics in biotechnology, computers, communications, software, micro-machines, and eco-technology, all impossible or difficult to see and difficult to verify by logic and science alone. Eco-technologies are incredibly varied, including agriculture and forestry biotechnology to increase yield, the genetic preservation of plant and animal species in gene pools and global gene registration centres, and the production of biochips (integrated circuits using living tissue) and biomechatronics (micro-machines based on the principles of living tissue), believed to be two of the most important technologies of the twenty-first century.

Asian countries particularly have attracted these Eco and multimedia technologies, rooted in the symbiosis of nature with science and technology. The development of information infrastructure and multimedia technology in countries such as Singapore and Malaysia are superior to those in the Western countries. Asian countries such as Japan and Malaysia are also treasure houses of the world's natural resources. The combination of natural and informational resources gives such Asian countries an overwhelming advantage over the West.

Fourthly, the twenty-first century order will be characterized by symbiosis among primary, secondary, and tertiary industry. For instance, agriculture once again will be a tremendous growth industry in the twenty-first century to provide food for a rocketing population, whose standard of living, even in developing countries, will improve. Meat consumption inevitably climbs when standards of living rise and grain consumption will skyrocket as feed for the livestock as well as for humans. Because of the demand for grain, China and the former Soviet Union, which until recently had been exporters of foodstuffs, have now become net importers. The only country exporting is the United States. Thus, humankind is in the extremely precarious position of relying wholly on American weather conditions and grain production.

The global foodstuff problem, particularly in Asia, cannot be resolved with conventional agriculture. A new type of agriculture is required that combines with secondary industries, such as the agricultural product processing industry and hydroponic cultivation, and tertiary industries, such as biotechnology and genetic engineering or even multimedia — for example, with an internet-based distribution and sales system. This can no longer be termed agriculture; it is more appropriately termed agri-industry.

The use of natural resources will also extend to leisure industries on an ever greater scale, responding to popular aspirations for a lifestyle that has a symbiotic relationship with nature. In addition to the current pattern of recreation, in which people head for the sea or the mountains in search of nature after their work is finished, people will build artificial forests and incorporate them in the cities. There will be a rapid growth in demand for living tress and bushes for the streets, parks and landscaping of cities, particularly.

It is clear then that architecture and urban planning will have to alter to meet these changing conditions. Without copying tradition, and by using contemporary building materials, we can create a new architecture and city of symbiosis. The Eco-Media City concept is a strategic project for realizing national and city planning for the twenty-first century based on the philosophy of symbiosis. Eco-Media cities will be sites for interaction between international society and the local community, and a locus for contact between the most modern experiments and daily life. An absolute condition for these metropolises will be to form comfortable, sophisticated urban amenities that enable globally-sophisticated people to gather, visit, and live there.

They will be the industrial cities of the twenty-first century, and will house R&D campuses, will be centres of exchange where international researchers, educators, artists, and cultural figures will be invited to live and interact with the population. They will be completely new, experimental cities open to the world, attracting new cutting-edge industries from inside and outside the country. But the cities will also preserve the natural environment by achieving a symbiosis of nature and the city, preservation and development, and nature and advanced technology through the more dynamic creation of forests and the effective use of natural resources. They will aim to become sustainable cities.

The cities will therefore experiment with a new style of living. They will become twenty-first century metropolises that provide an industrial base, living space, and a research environment for the information age. Conventional cities combined these functions and developed metropolises. The Eco-Media City concept, however, is of small-to medium-sized cities that form networks specializing in each of these functions (an R&D city, Expo City (Eco-City), Auto city, Sports City, High-tech City, Multi-media City, Aerospatial city etc.). Existing natural spaces, man-made forests, and farmland will lie between these cities. The network cities will coexist with nature and complement one another.

The information age will be a borderless era that links the world through a global information infrastructure (GII). Therefore, the Eco-Media cities will not become a reality if the construction of these infrastructures are limited to a single prefecture or single country. There must be a direct interlinkage through international hub airports, international hub ports and international information trunk lines.

In these Eco-Cities the flow of three different contents — information, people, and goods — will be intertwined in multi-level networks; that is, high-speed railways, expressways, logistics networks, and information networks (an information highway). This will result in the integration of people, goods, and information, to enable the establishment of a multimedia industry and an eco-media industry that utilizes natural resources, human resources (intellectual and creative abilities), goods and materials, and information (data content). If a multilevel network, and particularly a multimedia network, were compared to the trunk of a tree, the forest and natural areas surrounding a city would be like the leaves of a tree. The city is like the fruit that a tree produces at the ends of its branches, and an incubator for the production of information (content).

The first level of the infrastructure is a transportation network for people and the distribution system for goods. By 2025 we will experience a transport revolution for the coming era, when supersonic Mach 3.5 - 5.0 aircraft with 300-500 passengers will fly from New York to Tokyo in between three and five hours. By then airport runways will need to be at least 4,000 metres long to cater for such aircraft. It is said that the necessary number of such large-scale hub airports will be ten at most, with two in the Americas, two in Europe, three in Asia, one in the Middle East, one in Africa and one in Russia. There is no doubt that the cities with such large scale international hub airports will become hub cities in the twenty-first century, centres of finance, information, research and business. As part of their national strategy Malaysia, China and Korea are planning to build huge international hub airports by 2025.

Air cargo will see an increase even larger than that for passengers. Shipping container cargo is also increasing wordwide, particularly in Asia. It is expected that the twenty-first century will be an era of large 80,000 ton container ships, docking at large 15 metre deep hub ports. A design system must enable mutual access to the transportation infrastructure that links distribution centres capable of handling new types of port and airport freight, ports, and airports for handling the containerized freight predicted to come into wide use in the future. It will also include a logistics system (freight shipment network),and a computer control system that ships freight by the best and shortest possible route to factories using the just-in-time system.

The second infrastructure level is the information network, and infrastructure. This will require a high-speed, large-volume digital information infrastructure made of optical fibre. One such network already exists in the Internet, but other satellite and wireless networks are possible. Domestically, this multimedia network must be connected to every household (consumer) and company. Internationally, it must be connected to the GII through a linkage capable of high speeds and large content.

The third infrastructure level is ecological. An essential condition for the Eco-Media City is that it be a city of forests and plentiful natural spaces to foster the symbiosis between the development and the preservation of nature, and the symbiosis between eco-technology and multimedia technology. For example, the merger between nature, eco-technology and multimedia technology will require research and incubation facilities that enable joint research into biotechnology and multimedia technology. Natural resources and forests will also be a condition for the food processing industry and pharmaceutical industry that use eco-technologies such as biotechnology and genetic engineering. This means experimenting with ideas such as ecological corridors, and areas in which ecological systems and species can interact and communicate.

An extremely limited number of areas currently meet the conditions necessary to support Eco-Media cities. In the multimedia industry and the information infrastructure alone, the Western countries and Japan have an overwhelming lead in basic technology, related industries, and such human resources as researchers. It will be extremely difficult for the developing countries to catch up, and the first sophisticated multimedia cities will almost certainly be built in the United States and Japan.

Yet eco-technology also requires abundant natural resources, favourable climatic conditions, and water resources such as forests, forested mountains, rivers, seas, and lakes for Eco-Media cities to develop. Malaysia and other Asian coutries have an overwhelming advantage in these conditions for creating an Eco-Media industry and Eco-Media cities. The country in Asia with the most potential is Malaysia where the Multimedia Super Corridor project is being advanced under the leadership of its prime minister and which has an abundance of natural spaces, including a tropical rain forest, and the world's largest international hub airport and international hub port.

I am involved with planning Malaysia's new international hub airport with five runways, and the symbiotic metropolis, an Eco-Media City, which employs an information infrastructure. The new international hub airport is twice the size of the new Kansai International Airport. It will be one of the world's largest airports, and use the latest in high-tech equipment. Eco-Media City is slated to become the world's first experimental city that combines eco-technology and multimedia technology.

Major projects will also be under way for the next ten years in the Chubu region of Japan. This region also meets all the conditions for the Eco-Media city concept. The first phase of a new airport will be completed in this region by 2005. There will also be the Aichi Expo in 2005, the new Pacific National Traffic Axis, the Maglev Shinkansen, the renovation of the Nagoya and Yokkaichi harbours for the TSL (Techno-Super Liner) era, and the Tokai Beltway. It might also be possible to begin the Eco-Media city experiment in other Japanese regions, such as the Gifu Prefecture, Hyogo Prefecture, Mie Prefecture.

The Eco-Media city will become an entirely new concept for combining Eco-Technology and multimedia technology, promoting the symbiosis of the conservation of nature with development, and actively fulfilling its role in the global environment. It is the ultimate project for highlighting to the world the new age of symbiosis in which Asia is leading the way.

RIGHT: Factory (Benetton United Colours and Forms Research Centre), Treviso, Italy 1996. Photo Tadao Ando FAR RIGHT: Church of the Light, Osaka, 1989. Photo Mitsuo Matsuoka. BELOW: Naoshima Contemporary Art Museum, Annex Naoshima, 1995. Photo Shigeo Ogawa

Tadao Ando

Beyond Minimalism

As we enter the twenty-first century, we are all too aware of the rapid change taking place throughout the world, not only in the natural and man-made environments but also, and most importantly, in our sense of values. Countries around the globe are obsessed by economics and, deluded by the idea that wealth creation embodies high values, have embraced a lifestyle run by computers and informed unquestioningly by the mass media. We have lost sight of the truly important things in life.

If this trend continues, the differences between our cultures will be blended into a homogeneous uniformity which will destroy the characteristics and traditions that each nation or people has inherited. It will kill the sense of association to a specific region, the moral and spiritual character in its roots, and even the individual races themselves.

In the countries of the Asian region especially, the economy has been given the major emphasis in political and social policy. Material aspects have been unduly glorified; the indigenous culture, the traditions and history of each region have been ignored and even scorned. It would, however, be difficult to stem the flow of this trend which is running with the tide of the times. Even in architecture the volume of unnecessary information, the speed of its dissemination and the trend towards homogeneity, reinforced by economic reasoning, are a powerful presence. Architects must be consciously aware of these pressures and reflect on where their real responsibilities lie.

I should like to reaffirm that the most important aspect of architecture is its ability to move people with its poetic and creative power, and also to re-raise the question of whether architecture can be a true culture in and of itself. I should like to think that the interaction of architecture with nature can awaken and revive people's sensitivities through their physical being and their senses and can arouse in people the perceptiveness that they intrinsically possess. If we assume that what makes architecture true "Architecture" is not just a specific plan or design, not its relationship to technique or cost, but is the aesthetic expression of the architect's awareness of the issues involved, then the definition lies not only in architecture as a completed structure but within the process that is involved in its creation, in the manner in which architecture acquires life. The processes which take place before the architecture is born as form, while it is being converted into reality, and the change which occurs with time once it has been finished, are all a part of this act of creation. It is during that process of transition from poetic inspiration to the creation of form that the full range of an architect's ideas and thinking is brought into action. It is through repeated deliberation and contemplation, by searching every which way, by trial and error that the creative process which leads to architectural expression can be intensified and become more profound.

Thought is the realm where the soul and the spirit are one. The spirit is the core of the immeasurable; through a variety of processes thoughts are transformed into sketches, plans and drawings, and thus given expression. If, when my ideas or concepts progress – and within each line drawn, each number, each mark and symbol, or even the space in between, is injected the history, tradition, spiritual character and the sense of regional association to which my body and my five senses are deeply connected – if it can then acquire an eminence of aesthetic poetics, then I think it would truly become "architecture."

Twentieth-century architecture is made of techniques and materials – steel, concrete, glass, aluminium – that are common the world over. This tends to make buildings around the globe essentially the same and, like a dull and repetitious lifestyle, mundane and boring. It is incumbent on us to use the resources of our Earth in a more diverse manner; we should respect the unique lifestyles that are born from the differences in our cultures. I deliberately resist the idea of a "shrinking Earth."

There is no reason, despite its use of common materials and techniques, for modern architecture in Asian countries, the United Kingdom, Europe or the United States to be exactly the same and in an age of spreading digital information and globalisation, architects must address their responsibilities in a number of areas, the most important of which is what value we are to place on culture. The basis of culture is the moral and spiritual characteristics, the sensibilities, that a people has inherited through the ages. This is in addition to language and to the sense of association to nation or region. I therefore believe it is important that we use architecture to carry into the twenty-first century the covenant of culture that has been passed down to us through so much adversity.

In this period of accelerating globalisation we must make a conscious effort to preserve the peculiar language, the aesthetic values and the sensibilities that constitute the root of a culture as well as the almost unconscious physical habits that we inherit and use in our daily lives and also the craftsmanship that is handed down to us, all of which may be considered to be the true strength and power of a people. Language is deeply connected to a people's moral and spiritual make-up; writing and speaking in that language determine their form of expression.

For a piece of architecture to possess a universality that is understood through a common consciousness in people of all races and beliefs, it must be understood through the process of thought and planning that takes place before its completion. The intrinsic culture, tradition, history, the moral and spiritual character of a people is intimately entwined in the process of deliberation and will determine whether or not the architect's understanding of these issues will reach the heights of architectural expression. Thus do I reaffirm my conviction that any consideration of architecture must be centred on the process of creation itself.

Günter Nitschke

Chinju no mori – Urban Deity Groves

Western observers do not seem to understand the modern Japanese city. To their untrained eyes the Japanese city is Janus-faced. Either it is visually chaotic and amorphous, or it is socially vital, efficient, and safe. But the European aesthetic and social values behind this view of the Japanese city, are inappropriate. The Japanese city has a different structure, and the Japanese an altogether different spatial culture.

I began to reveal elsewhere[1] the hidden hands which have historically structured the Japanese city by isolating two of its fundamental features. The first, the Japanese sense of community, is spatially expressed in the *chō* the basic unit of the neighbourhood group. This system of the *chō* seems to be the only alternative to the system of street names and numbers used by the rest of the world for urban orientation. Tokyo may be the largest city on the globe, but it has no street names and numbers. The second feature, the Japanese sense of urban trade, is spatially expressed in the *kaiwai*, the commercial district.

But there is a third hidden hand, the *chinju no mori*, or urban deity groves, perhaps the closest functional equivalent in Japan to the religious or civic squares of Europe. The West has always assumed that the Japanese city lacks civic or market squares and spaces. It is true that traditionally there has been no real social need for Western-style civic squares in Japan. Where they have been introduced as copies of European precedents, such as in Kyoto, south of its city hall, they have proved to be eyesores, ending up as open-air car-parks. The squares in front of railway stations, introduced in Meiji times and reconstructed after World War II, are little better, simply traffic islands cluttered with vehicles. Likewise you will not find Japanese markets and shops on squares and piazzas. Instead, Japanese markets usually line city streets or processional paths leading up to Shinto shrines or Buddhist temples, And the longer and narrower these shopping streets are, the more shoppers they attract. The famous Nishiki Market in downtown Kyoto, for example, is just 2.8m wide, but 600m long.

It is not surprising that the West has overlooked the urban deity groves as equivalents of civic squares. To the untrained eye they appear to be very different, more like parks, scattered like green oases in the tightly packed jigsaw puzzle of the Japanese city. Yet these groves, more than any other urban form, hold the key to understanding the deep-seated Japanese sense of belonging not only to a group of people, but to a particular plot of land. The *chinju no mori* and their surrounding neighbourhoods define another type of neighbourhood group, a sacred one, which is superimposed on and subsumes all other social groupings.

The groves still function today as religious and civic landmarks within cities and villages.[2] They consist of at least one shrine building, if not several, intimately connected to its processional approach, the *sando*, marked by one or many consecutive *torii*, or typical Shinto gates. They also contain a covered dance hall, a place for washing with fresh water, and a purification space laid out with white gravel. A grove of trees contains the whole ensemble, setting it apart from the surrounding secular urban fabric.[3]

They have an ancient and complex history.[4] In the earliest prehistoric phase of Shinto, known as "Nature Shinto," the Japanese venerated their deities at the foot of mountains or beside rivers. They would place sanctuaries there, often consisting of empty ground laid out with river pebbles. In early spring a combined Mountain-Field-Ancestor Deity would be magically called down into a temporary shrine, a *yori-shiro*, erected on this pebbled ground.[5] This temporary shrine would be made of simply a tree or perhaps just a branch brought down from the nearest mountain. A liturgical address would be followed by the dedication of simple agricultural offerings, and dances performed to amuse the deity. Then at the end of this rite of renewal, called the *matsuri*, the deity would be magically sent away, often by destroying the sacred shrine itself.

In the next stage of Shinto, known as "Storehouse Shinto," the offerings had become so elaborate that a simple storage hall had to be built to house them. Eventually these halls, as well as the offerings they contained, were ritually renewed as well, becoming an integral and sacred part of the annual festival. By the seventh century, and the final phase of Shinto, known as "Shrine Building Shinto," the offerings themselves had come to be seen as the *go-shintai*, or the deity's body itself; and what were once simply temporary storehouses for divine offerings had become built increasingly as permanent residences for the deities, so that they could be venerated at any time, not only during the festivals,

Having become, in effect, permanent buildings, the architecture of Shinto shrine buildings was able to develop. At the outset shrine buildings, apart from a few exceptions such as the Ise, Izumo or Sumiyoshi shrines, were constructed along the lines of imported Buddhist temple architecture, borrowing their general spatial order and formal language. Gradually the architecture of the shrines fused with that of the Buddhist temples. This was prompted by a unification of Shinto deities and Buddhas, called *shimbutsu shugo*, based on the ancient Buddhist philosophy of assimilation, by which native deities of any country into which Buddhism spread become adopted as just manifestations of the true nature of Buddhas and Boddhisatvas.[6] As a result, from the early middle ages to the nineteenth century Shinto shrines and Buddhist temples largely shared the same sanctuary. Even today the Japanese see no problem in this. Most of life's happy events are performed in Shinto shrines, most unhappy ones in Buddhist

ABOVE: Late 18th-century woodcut of crowd waiting on both sides of the approach to the Gion Shrine in Kyoto for the Mikoshi to be brought out. BELOW: Dance hall (front) and Deity Hall (back) of Shimo Goryō Shrine. OVERLEAF: Portable shrine palanquin taken out of the shrine precinct of Shimo Goryō Shrine at the climax of the festival.

temples. The latter, like Christian churches, have cemeteries attached to their precincts, Shinto shrines never. This physical coexistence has bred a similar coexistence of both religions in the hearts of the Japanese.

However, Shinto shrines and Buddhist temples were segregated by law in 1868. In 1871 Shinto shrines were re-classified and in 1880 a shrine count was undertaken: there were 123 *kansha*, or central government shrines and 186,688 *minsha*, or people's shrines, from prefectural shrines to the smallest ungraded ones. At first the Meiji Government tried to promote Shinto as the state religion with a divine emperor as the head of a state conceived as a *koku-tai*, a "national body." It tried to control all shrines, in particular the "people's shrines." When these efforts failed because of concerns about

religious freedom, the government suddenly switched policy and began to promote shrines as non-religious but patriotic institutions. Massive shrine mergers were undertaken, with the official aim of clearing shrines unbefitting their new role. But the real aim was to use them as instruments of propaganda for new nationalist goals and for consolidating popular loyalty to the emperor. The mergers were simple to arrange: the *go-shintai* were simply removed and the grove of trees cut down. In this way over forty per cent of all village and ungraded shrines were destroyed between 1906 and 1920.[7]

In the huge wave of urban sprawl that swept Japan from the 1950s to the 1980s many village communities were swallowed up by the expanding city limits, and with them many *chinju no mori*. There remain today perhaps 106,000 groves, that is one per 1,000 people. Yet their power over urban form is still strong. Even today, travelling by train at 250 kilometres an hour along the eastern coast, you can spy dots of green throughout the monotonous, linear megacity – these are the *chinju no mori*. If you stop to visit one of these deity-groves today, you can still see in their physical form a reminder of the "Storehouse Shinto" phase of shrine building. They still look very much like solid storages boxes without windows – appropriately so since they contain the *go-shintai* and usually various precious offerings and adornments. They are are always fenced in and are generally inaccessible to the ordinary believer. By contrast, a Buddhist temple can always be entered and its sacred artefact, the Buddhist idol, is usually visible.

But there is an even stronger echo of the past, of the very first phase of Shinto, the "Nature Shinto" phase – the trees. The shrines' setting in a grove of trees is a reminder of "natural" nature, as it were, and today the highest possible offering to one's deity at any Shinto ritual is still a branch of the sakaki tree, an evergreen sacred to Shinto. Trees weave through the deity groves in every way. Etymologically, *mori* is either written with the Chinese character for a birch-leaf pear tree or that for a forest picturing three trees; linguistically its meanings include "to guard," "plentiful," and "a place abounding in trees," all of which perfectly describe these Shinto shrines. The integration of trees actually and metaphorically represents perfectly the binding together of place, spirit and nature. Initially, Shinto deities were believed to be directly related to the powers of natural phenomena, or to the spirits of one's kin and ancestors, to one's occupation, and to the energies of the very ground they stood on. In other words they were believed to be genius loci, very close to our current understanding of the term.[8]

However, from the fourteenth century, as basic settlements developed in Japan, the deities came to be regarded as the guardians of local co-operative communities too, known as *uji-gami*.[9] So they became assimilated in local civic ritual. For instance, during the *Matsuri*,[11] the shrine's rite of renewal, a *chinju no mori* and its *sando*, or approach, suddenly turns into a festival, a buzzing market place. Shrine supporters from the surrounding *chō* contribute gifts of wine and money and gather to see and possibly touch the *Mikoshi*, the portable shrine containing the deity's body during the festival. The deity is carried in a festive, often wild procession encircling and crossing its sacred territory, blessing its *ujiko*, or "chosen people." For the rest of the year the Shinto deity groves serve as civic meeting places, places to greet the New Year or present one's new-born children to one's guardian deities, places for children to play in, or simply as places for a moment's silent prayer. Throughout all this activity, though, their form is always protected. In Shinto belief the *chinju no mori* as a whole is believed to be part of the deity's body, and therefore, as sacred. No trees can be cut or even tampered with easily.

It is Shinto, laced as it is through Japanese culture, that holds the key to the true nature of the groves. Shinto is not a religion in the Western sense; rather it is an early human insight into nature and the human being, somehow a foreshadowing of contemporary ideas of Gaia, of the earth as a living, conscious organism. The *chinju no mori* represent the perennial values of Japanese culture rooted in Shinto, values which somehow complement the dominant Western ones. The Japanese, deep in their soul, have a clear predisposition for a culture of movement and flow rather than statics and the material. They crave the alive and the raw rather than the cooked in their cuisine. They love "natural" ambiguity and abhor intellectual clarity in both their literature and daily language. In education and social etiquette they prefer merging into a group to sticking out as individuals. In architecture the ephemeral and seasonal is valued above the enduring and monumental. And in their cities and towns the creation of a vital chaos is preferred to aesthetic order. Look again at the aerial photo of Osaka; this city view is no exception in Japan; it is the norm. The amorphous competitive city has always been both the ideal and reality in Japan. The Japanese city is more a jungle than a garden.

So the Western observers are wrong when they claim that there is no civic place in Japanese cities. They have, armed with the bias of their own culture, simply looked for it in the wrong place. Whereas Europeans have traditionally built civic spaces as rather hard, stone piazzas, as bright open spaces surrounded by weighty buildings, the Japanese have built theirs as soft and mysterious gardens, as dim and natural groves of trees which change with the seasons. The Europeans choose inert materials, the Japanese ones that are alive. The former try to outwit time by building with materials assumed to be permanent, the latter tries to do the same but by the mechanism of renewal.[12] Similarly in building cities Western culture is obsessed with the quest for the the City Beautiful, the City Eternal. Japan, though, is searching for the Vital City, one ever renewing itself.

In this renewal the groves remain a vital inspiration – for new architecture too. Even that latest and ultimate fin-de-siècle statement of post-postmodern high-tech architecture in Japan, Hiroshi Hara's Kyoto Station Complex, perhaps the largest in the world, can easily be interpreted as a profane version of a traditional Shinto sanctuary on a steep slope. And there are hundreds more of them in Japan. The spatial order displayed in both these sacred and profane "shrines" is the same: one ascends, via enormous stairs (admittedly escalators in Hara's design) to ever higher platforms, which reveal ever more breathtaking views to the visitor. The oscillation between movement and rest, stairs and platforms lures the visitor ever onward, seemingly up to the clouds. The only difference lies in their use. In Shinto shrine precincts one proceeds to and arrives at ever more sacred places and shrines. In Hara's station building one moves from one level of shops, coffee houses and restaurants to the next. The gods worshipped may have changed, but the popularity of their places remains the same.

This essay appeared in an earlier version in *DAIDALOS 67*, 1997.

[1] Nitschke, Günter, "From Ambiguity to Transparency – The unperspective, perspective, and aperspective paradigm of space," Copenhagen: Louisiana Revy, Vol. 35, No. 3, 1995.
[2] For a rare English exposition of the ten most important *chinju no mori* chosen to protect the new Meiji capital of Tokyo see Nakajima, Takeo "Spatial Composition of the Shrine," in *Process Architecture* 25, 1981, and Jinnai, Hidenoby "Ethnic Tokyo," in *Process Architecture* 72, 1991.
[3] Ueda, Atsushi, (ed.) *chinju no mori* (Guardian Deity Groves), Tokyo: Kashima Shuppankai, 1984. See also Kato, Akinori, *toshi no hiroba chinju no mori koen* (Parks of Deity Groves as Urban Squares). *in midori no bummei* (The Culture of Green), Tokyo: Midori no bummeisha, 86.
[4] An illustrated version of such a historical overview can be found in the author's "Daijosai and Shikinen Sengu – First Fruits Twice Tasted," in *From Shinto to Ando*, London: Academy Editions, 1993.
[5] For a more detailed discussion of those terms and their forms see the author's "SHIME - Binding/Unbinding," London: *Architectural Design* 12, 1974.
[6] A thorough study of this highly complex process of assimilation of Shinto and Buddhism in Japan, in philosophy and iconography, is *The Buddhist Philosophy of Assimilation*, by Matsunaga, Alicia, Tokyo: Sophia University, 1969.
[7] All data on Meiji era Shinto are taken from Fridel, Wilburn M., *Japanese Shrine Mergers 1906-1912*, Tokyo: Sophia University, 1973.
[8] Norberg-Schulz, *Genius Loci*, New York: Rizzoli, 1980.
[9] Still the best essay on the relationship between *uji-gami*, Clan Deities and *matsuri*, Rites of Renewal, is found in "The Development of Matsuri" by Harada, Toshiaki, in *Philosophical Studies of Japan*, Vol.II, 1960.
[10] Summarized from Ueda, 1984, pp. 31-32.
[11] In ancient Japanese the term *matsuri* stood for Shinto Festival, as well as Government Affairs, pointing to a conceptual identity between religious and civic affairs. Shinto, originally, was very much a mixture of an all-encompassing true ecological and civic religion.
[12] The exploration of these values and their manifestation in Japanese architecture and towns is the theme of a fascinating small book by Ueda, Atsushi, *nihon no toshi wa umi kara tsukurareta*, ("Japanese Cities were conceived and built from the Sea"), Tokyo: Chuo-koronsha, 1996.

Evelyn Schulz

A Confucian Critique of Modern Tokyo and its Future: Kōda Rohan's "One Nation's Capital"[1]

Introduction

Attempts have been made in the West to rethink the Enlightenment and to abandon all universal concepts. Now people prefer to speak of "global modernities" rather than of one single path to modernity.[2] Those engaged in urban discourse emphasize that there is no definition of the city that is independent of its cultural background, and nor can a clear-cut method for analyzing the city as an abstract, universal concept be developed.[3] In modern Japan reflection upon the city is even more complicated than in the West, because the discourse is polarized between East and West on the one hand and between tradition and modernity on the other. Definitions rooted in an American or West-European context can nevertheless be helpful tools for analyzing urban matters in other cultures if one keeps their limits in mind.

Kōda Rohan's (1867-1947) conception of Tokyo as revealed in *Ikkoku no shuto* (*One Nation's Capital*), published in 1899, reflects the problem of the conceptualization of the city as an abstract idea. Rohan analyzes Tokyo's modernization during the Meiji period and the problems emanating from its new function as the national capital and from its growth following the tremendous increase in population caused by migration and industrialization.

Tokyo's situation at the turn of the century

Owing to the abolition of the *sankin kotai* (alternate attendance)[4] in 1862 and the turmoil in the years around the Meiji Restoration in 1868, more than half of Tokyo's inhabitants left the city and returned to their hometowns. Only 500,000 people remained. It was not until the 1890s that Tokyo regained the population of Edo at its peak – more than one million people. By the turn of the century it already had a population of 1.4 million.

In the age of imperialism cities were regarded as symbols of the progress of mankind and as the embodiment of modern civilization. Capital cities represent the nation. On the one hand they are objects of ambitious city planning, on the other they are targets of social and political criticism. Meiji Japan, like Victorian England and like Germany, adapted the ideology of progress and produced images of historical, and hence cultural continuity in architecture.

Following the models of Paris and Berlin, Tokyo was in the process of being modernized. Improvements to Tokyo's infrastructure were a very urgent problem. The city's population suffered from the lack of a sewage system, from overpopulation and diseases, and from the permanent danger of fire. The government designed a new city centre with the aim of having it represent the nation's identity and the government's authority. The new Tokyo was to represent Japan as a nation-state. It was to become a symbol of Japan's participation in the competition of the "enlightened," "civilized" nations of the West.

Most of the people who were involved in the modernization projects had a mechanistic view of the city. The emphasis was on the construction of a representative capital through monumental architecture, broad avenues, and public spaces. Tokyo's modernization was a challenge to be met with modern technology. The question of the citizen's function within the process of social reorganization which accompanied the rebuilding of the city did not appear in the considerations at all.

Rohan's *One Nation's Capital*

Rohan's treatise can be read as a criticism of this view of the city. He argues against two positions: he criticizes both the conservative sentimentalists who longed for old Edo and concentrated on the evocation of the past instead of creating a vision of Tokyo's future; and the government's technocratic policy for Tokyo's reorganization.

Surprisingly, in *One Nation's Capital* there are no descriptions of architecture or streets. Rohan's concern is Tokyo's social modernization. He therefore focuses on the people who live in Tokyo and make up the urban community. He perceives the city as a living subject. He sees every part of it as connected with the other parts and all parts as dependent on each other, similar to a living organism. On the basis of this image he creates a correlation of state, capital city, and citizen. Thus his criticism encompasses not only Tokyo but the whole nation.

Although *One Nation's Capital* is not divided into chapters, three related parts can be distinguished:

In the first part of the text Rohan asks what constitutes a capital city in general. What is its relationship to the country and the periphery? And what should be the basis for the citizen's relationship to the city? Here Rohan's thoughts focus on the future and reflect Western ideas such as those of the individual, community, and society. The terms he uses to express these ideas are neologisms coined during the Meiji period, such as *shakai* (society), or categories of pre-modern Japanese thought such as *jikaku* (self-awareness), originally a Buddhist term which during the Meiji period came to be an important tool for discussing the Western idea of the individual.

In the middle part, Rohan describes new elements of the city's infrastructure such as the organization of waste removal, a sewage system and of communal institutions such as public parks and kindergartens.

The last part of *One Nation's Capital* differs in important aspects from the other parts. Here Rohan outlines the history of Edo's pleasure districts and its prospering popular culture and he states that they caused Edo's decline because of their negative influence on the inhabitants' morals. Thus, the history of Edo becomes a history of moral decline. This judgement forms the background of his whole criticism. From this vantage point he warns that Tokyo might decline like Edo did, and he attempts to make proposals about how Tokyo's history could become a history of success and prosperity.

Images of Tokyo in Rohan's *One Nation's Capital*
Tokyo as chaos
For Rohan Tokyo is in every respect in a state of "chaos" (*konton*) and looks like an "unfinished product" (*miseihin*). He states that even the idea of what the capital city should be is "chaotic and without shape" (*konton musho*). In Taoist thought "chaos" (in Chinese *hundun*; In Japanese *konton*) is a central term and means a condition "that has its own internal principles of organization, change, order, and life." In this respect it shares similarities with the current discourse on chaos theory in natural sciences and in city planning.[5] The image of chaos is Rohan's tool to depict the city as being in a state of permanent change and flux.

During the Meiji period "chaos" (*konton*) not only had a Taoist connotation but was also an important term in the discourse on civilization which was deeply influenced by the Western theory of progress, by Positivism and Social Darwinism. There *konton* has a completely different meaning than it has in Taoism. It means primitive chaos and points to the lowest stage of barbarism.[6] Applied to Tokyo as depicted in *One Nation's Capital* "chaos" means "not yet civilized." In Rohan's view Tokyo had not yet been formed.

Tokyo as an organism
In contrast to the image of chaos that serves to describe Tokyo's condition, the image of an organism forms the matrix of Rohan's discussion of the central functions that in his opinion the capital city has to fulfil. Rohan focuses on the function of the city as a social organism.

Conceiving the city by making analogies to the proportions of the human body has a long tradition in European thought.[7] But it seems that especially during the nineteenth and twentieth centuries the image of the city as an organism gained new meaning. Because of the tremendous growth in population the size of the city lost every link to anthropometrical proportions. Now a city conceived of as an organism came to mean seeing it as a living being and applying to it such characteristics as movement and diversity in order to cope conceptually with its growing size and changing structure.

Furthermore, the image of an organism was a useful tool to discuss the city in social and political terms both in the West and in Japan. In the political thought of the nineteenth century it implies the correlation between city, urban society, and nation.[8] Rohan writes: A nation's "capital" (*shuto*) is like a human head. It is equipped with all kinds of high-grade facilities and is the place where all activities arise and where they return.

Rohan describes Tokyo's condition mainly on the basis of aesthetic categories that are deeply rooted in Confucian thought. The city is not a machine that can be reformed merely through modern technology. It is an organism that has to become "good" from the inside. In Confucian thought the "good" (*zen*) means shape, system, order, and harmony. The binary terms "good" (*zen/zenbi*) and "bad" (*aku*) are Rohan's means of judging Tokyo's state in aesthetic, moral and hygienic terms. In his opinion the city is "bad" at present and requires the "good" for its future.

In Rohan's view there are two reasons for the decline of the city (*tofu no suiraku*): the citizens' passive attitude towards the city and egoism that does not care for anything but personal matters. Tokyo's prosperity rests not only upon the buildings but also depends on the people's emotions for the city (13). In order to improve, Tokyo needs its citizens' "love" (*ai*). *Ai* is a central term in Confucian thought. Rohan makes the city a beloved object through anthropomorphization and thus reduces the emotional distance between city and citizens.

Community and citizen
Chaos and organism share common characteristics: both are always in flux. Because of migration into the city and the evolution of new social structures after the abolition of the feudal system, Tokyo's citizens were a mixture of people who had lived there before and people who had come from all over the country. Rohan regards the diversity of Tokyo's population in a very positive light: the city is a place where individuals have countless possibilities for contact with each other. In Rohan's view the amalgamation of their thoughts will create a new consciousness of the city. Finally, it is the citizen who creates the city.

The Western idea of the autonomous individual had an enormous impact on the Meiji discourse on civilization. The question of what individuals should be and how their relationship to the state was supposed to be was one of the most discussed topics in Meiji intellectual discourse and can be found in nearly every text on society, culture, and philosophy. Special to Rohan's considerations is the fact that he extends the idea of the individual to the urban citizen who is equipped with a sense of responsibility towards the community where he lives.

The three "powers" that according to Rohan make up the country, the "power of wealth" (*furyoku*), the "power of virtue" (*tokuryoku*), and the "power of knowledge" (*chiryoku*), can also be regarded as the main characteristics of the new citizens. Rohan summarizes their predominant characteristics with the term *jikaku* ((self-)awareness or (self-)awakening). For Rohan *jikaku* means "real knowledge, real morality, and real emotion" (31). It appears as the magic formula for Tokyo's social reorganization. According to Rohan, *jikaku* creates "ideals" (*riso*) and "faith" (*shinko*) (47). Both combine to form a "purposeful movement" that "facing the light [will] advance" (*komei ni mukatte o susumuru*) (47-48). The aim of such movement is a "capital city that is alive" (*inochi aru shuto*) and changing day by day (48).

Conclusion

One Nation's Capital is an appeal to reform Tokyo. Rohan outlines the functions of the new national capital. The text can be read as an attempt to overcome the alienation Japan's modernization had caused the individual with the idea of a new urban community. His thoughts on the urban community have similarities with those of contemporary social thinkers in East and West (Kang Youwei, Ebenezer Howard, Ferdinand Tönnies). This amalgamation of ideas rooted in different cultures reflects the general circumstances of Meiji intellectual discourse. The intellectuals perceived their age as a time of transition and had to cope conceptually with great social and cultural change and diversity. Thus, in Rohan's treatise images of Tokyo as chaos and organism appear as appro-priate means to perceive the city where most of these changes took place.

Apart from the convincing modernity of Rohan's ideas, his way of presenting his arguments, their structure and moralizing diction, recall classical Chinese rhetorics such as those used in *Daxue* (Japanese *Daigaku*, the Great Learning). His criticism is based on the construction of a polarity between Edo and Tokyo. In *One Nation's Capital*, Edo and Tokyo are depicted as two different cities. Rohan emphasizes the discontinuities caused by the Meiji reforms. Both in the West and in Japan the description of urban phenomena was (and still is) a tool for social and political criticism of modernity and of modernization in general. In the Japanese paradigm of criticism of modernity it is a common feature to use the split in Tokyo's history as an instrument for criticising the changes brought by the Meiji reforms against the background of its past. It is astonishing how deterministic and inflexible Rohan's image of history is. In this respect *One Nation's Capital* is not a universal treatise on the modern city. In line with Confucianism: Rohan refers to the real and to the concrete, namely Tokyo, the city where he lives. The autonomous individual disappears from his thoughts. His view of history follows the pattern of a "history of decline" which is rooted in Chinese thought. Rohan seems not to show the slightest interest in all the factors that determined politics towards the end of the Edo period, for instance, the tremendous social problems or the pressure from outside. In Rohan's criticism the history of Edo is a history of moral decline and Edo serves as the negative model for Tokyo's future.

One Nation's Capital can also be seen as a manifesto of Confucian thinking in the modern age. Probably Rohan wanted to show that cate-gories such as "love" (*ai* or *aijo*), "virtue" (*toku*) and "knowledge" (*chi*), which stem from Chinese thought, are not only still valid for the des-cription of modern phenomena and for the conception of the future of the capital, but that they gain importance in the face of the alienation of modern urban society. But viewed from the present, Rohan's thought lacked the instruments needed to cope with modern urban phenomena.

Bibliography

Blacker, Carmen (1964). *The Japanese Enlightenment. A Study of the Writings of Fukuzawa Yukichi.* Cambridge University Press.

Featherstone, Michael, Lash, Scott and Roland Robertson (ed.) (1995). *Global Modernities.* London, SAGE Publications.

Girardot, N. J. (1983). *Myth and Meaning in Early Taoism. The Theme of Chaos (hun-tun).* Berkeley, University of California Press.

Ko̅da [Kouda] Rohan (1993). *Ikkoku no shuto.* Tokyo, Iwanami shoten.

Kruft, Hanno-Walter (1991). *Geschichte der Architekturtheorie.* Von der Antike bis zur Gegenwart. Munich, Beck.

Lees, Andrew (1984). "The Metropolis and the Intellectual." In: Sutcliffe, Anthony (ed.). *Metropolis 1890-1940.* Mansell, Alexandrine Press, pp. 67-94.

Mayer, Henry M. (1971). "Definitions of 'City.'" In: Bourne, Larry Stuart. *The Internal Structure of the City.* Oxford University Press, pp. 28-31.

Schumann, Ulrich Maximilian (1995). "Die Freiheit zu bauen. Bürgerarchitektur des 19. und 20. Jahrhunderts." In: Salden, Hubert (ed.). *Die Städelschule Frankfurt am Main von 1817 bis 1995.* Ausstellungskatalog Städelsches Kunstinstitut Frankfurt/M., pp. 95-121.

Sennett, Richard (1994). *Flesh and Stone. The Body and the City in Western Civilization.* New York, Norton.

Smith, Henry D. (1978). "Tokyo as an idea: An exploration of Japanese urban thought until 1945." In: *Journal of Japanese Studies*, Summer 1978, Vol. 4, No. 2, pp. 45-80.

Taut, Bruno (1995). "Die Stadtkrone." In: Lampugnani, Vittorio Magnago. *Texte zur Geschichte des Städtebaus. Band IV. 20. Jahrhundert. Tradition und Avantgarde.* Zürich: Eidgenössische Technische Hochschule, pp. 93-100, (1919).

Tönnies, Ferdinand (1995). "Gemeinschaft und Gesellschaft." In: Lampugnani, Vittorio Magnago. *Texte zur Geschichte des Städtebaus. Band IV. 20. Jahrhundert. Tradi-tion und Avantgarde.* Zürich: Eidgenössische Technische Hochschule, pp. 123-128, (1887).

Zibell, Barbara (1995). *Chaos als Ordnungsprinzip im Städtebau. Ansätze zu einem neuen Planungsverständnis.* Zürich: vdf Hochschulverlag (ORL-Bericht 99/1995).

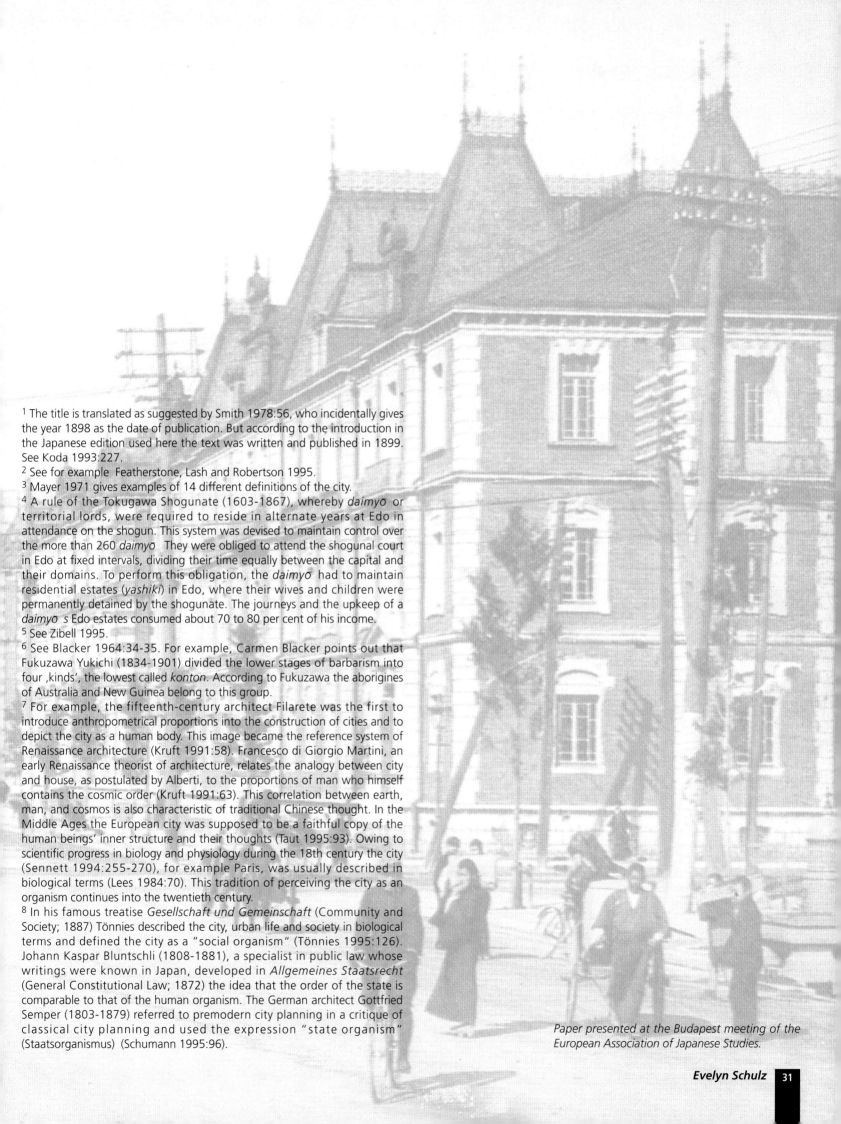

[1] The title is translated as suggested by Smith 1978:56, who incidentally gives the year 1898 as the date of publication. But according to the introduction in the Japanese edition used here the text was written and published in 1899. See Koda 1993:227.

[2] See for example Featherstone, Lash and Robertson 1995.

[3] Mayer 1971 gives examples of 14 different definitions of the city.

[4] A rule of the Tokugawa Shogunate (1603-1867), whereby daimyō or territorial lords, were required to reside in alternate years at Edo in attendance on the shogun. This system was devised to maintain control over the more than 260 daimyō They were obliged to attend the shogunal court in Edo at fixed intervals, dividing their time equally between the capital and their domains. To perform this obligation, the daimyō had to maintain residential estates (yashiki) in Edo, where their wives and children were permanently detained by the shogunate. The journeys and the upkeep of a daimyō s Edo estates consumed about 70 to 80 per cent of his income.

[5] See Zibell 1995.

[6] See Blacker 1964:34-35. For example, Carmen Blacker points out that Fukuzawa Yukichi (1834-1901) divided the lower stages of barbarism into four ‚kinds', the lowest called konton. According to Fukuzawa the aborigines of Australia and New Guinea belong to this group.

[7] For example, the fifteenth-century architect Filarete was the first to introduce anthropometrical proportions into the construction of cities and to depict the city as a human body. This image became the reference system of Renaissance architecture (Kruft 1991:58). Francesco di Giorgio Martini, an early Renaissance theorist of architecture, relates the analogy between city and house, as postulated by Alberti, to the proportions of man who himself contains the cosmic order (Kruft 1991:63). This correlation between earth, man, and cosmos is also characteristic of traditional Chinese thought. In the Middle Ages the European city was supposed to be a faithful copy of the human beings' inner structure and their thoughts (Taut 1995:93). Owing to scientific progress in biology and physiology during the 18th century the city (Sennett 1994:255-270), for example Paris, was usually described in biological terms (Lees 1984:70). This tradition of perceiving the city as an organism continues into the twentieth century.

[8] In his famous treatise Gesellschaft und Gemeinschaft (Community and Society; 1887) Tönnies described the city, urban life and society in biological terms and defined the city as a "social organism" (Tönnies 1995:126). Johann Kaspar Bluntschli (1808-1881), a specialist in public law whose writings were known in Japan, developed in Allgemeines Staatsrecht (General Constitutional Law; 1872) the idea that the order of the state is comparable to that of the human organism. The German architect Gottfried Semper (1803-1879) referred to premodern city planning in a critique of classical city planning and used the expression "state organism" (Staatsorganismus) (Schumann 1995:96).

Paper presented at the Budapest meeting of the European Association of Japanese Studies.

Toyo Ito and Takenaka Corporation

The Odate Jukai Dome

The Odate Jukai Dome was designed jointly by Toyo Ito & Associates and the Takenaka Corporation as a core facility for the sports and recreation concepts promoted by Odate City and its surrounding towns. It is a large multi-purpose facility for use throughout the year, as it is unaffected by the severe cold and snowfalls of winter.

The dome is designed to blend in with the environment. The hope is that the architecture of materials and forms born from nature will once again assimilate itself into the surrounding nature to create a new natural environment. For example, the egg-shaped structure is designed to align with the prevailing winds, and to cope with heavy snowfalls. Its beautiful roof is made from Akita cedar from local sources. Its double-layer construction encloses an internal space brightly illuminated by natural light. These considerations made the construction, detailed design and execution of the work both complex and difficult. But the efforts were worthwhile because the completed structure not only copes with these functional demands but does so in a beautiful design, which, from every angle, continually stimulates the viewer at all hours of the day.

Structural Design

The roof structure consists of a two-arch truss with a depth of 3m to 5m along the longer side, and a single-layer arch along the shorter side, which are reciprocally assembled to form a grillage-type structure along the plane. The two-directional arch uniformly resists a snow load equivalent to twice the weight of the roof. In addition, the truss along the longer side restricts deformation, preventing the structure from buckling.

The assembly of upper/lower chord members of the arched truss along the longer side (forming the grillage and the principal members of the arch along the shorter side) brings out clearly the soothing effect of the wood. At the same time the tying members, diagonal members and in-lane members have a pleasant "steel" effect, giving an overall impression of blending well with the finished roof members.

Ecological Design

The dome's design aims to use natural resources efficiently. The double-layer construction of the roof allows the dispersed, natural light to strike all corners and brightly illuminate the internal space. The design also prevents condensation in winter and absorbs sound. It is hoped that the dome will provide a comfortable and cool environment in whatever weather, by using mainly natural air. At noon during summer the south-west side facing the direction of the prevailing winds takes in external air, which is cooled naturally by the pond installed in the front, and through sliding sashes at the foot of the structure. This cooled wind eliminates any heat in the dome. The openings at the foot and all around the structure are located at different heights, and even when there is no wind, they ventilate the internal space effectively. Furthermore, by opening the vents provided on top of the roof, the heat accumulated in the upper part of the large space can be expelled outside. During winter, the space is heated by blowing hot air from below the bench seats. The pond installed outside the dome can store rain water which, with well water, is used for flushing toilets, for sprinkling on plants and for melting snow.

Design:
Toyo Ito & Associates, Architects
and Takenaka Corporation,
in collaboration with
Hirohiko Hangai (structure),
L.P.A. (lighting plan), and
Kijuro Yahagi Co. Ltd. (signage)

Construction:
Takenaka Corporation

Site:
Kamidaino Ohdate, Akita prefecture

Site area:
110,250.65 sq.m.

Function:
Pitch for baseball and other sports

Building area:
21,910.65 sq.m.

Floor area:
23,218.40 sq.m;

Building height:
52m

Seating:
Infield 3,520
(fixed 2,120; movable 1,400)
Outfield 1,520

Design period:
1993-1995

Construction:
1995-1997

Photographer:
Mikio Kamaya

PAGE 32: Computer-generated exploded axonometry
LEFT: The Odate Jukai Dome as seen from the
surrounding landscape
BELOW: The Odate Jukai Dome, interior detail
OPPOSITE
RIGHT: The Odate Jukai Dome, sketch by Toyo Ito
BELOW: The Odate Jukai Dome, exterior detail of dome

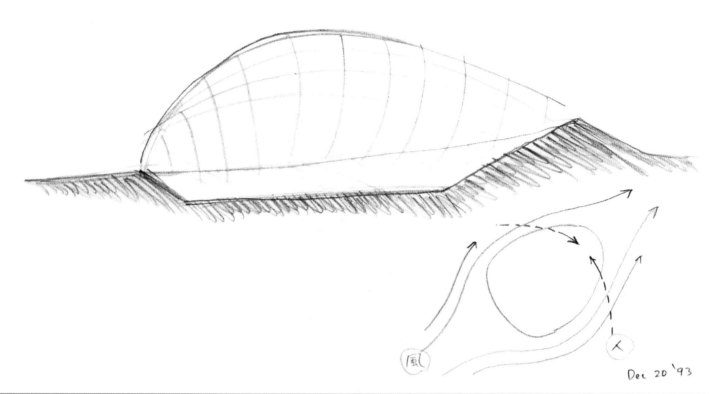

風　人　Dec 20 '93

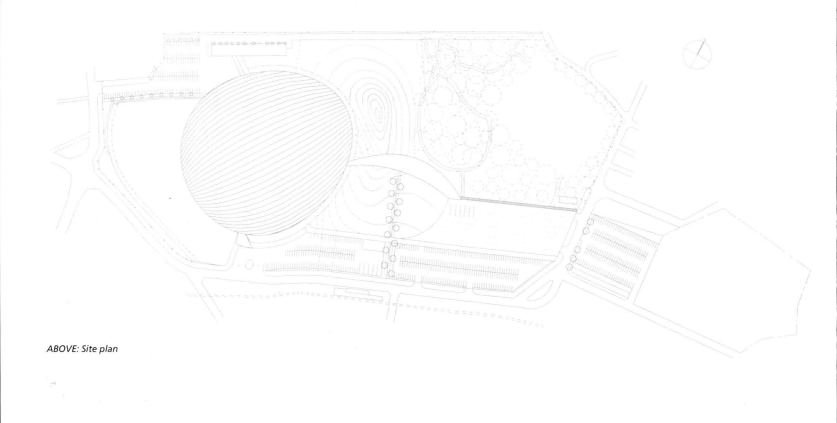

ABOVE: Site plan

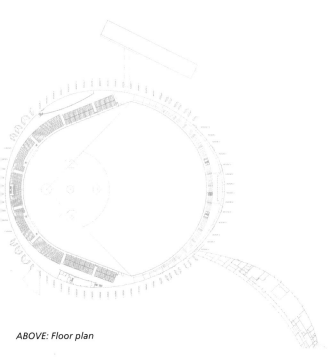

ABOVE: Floor plan

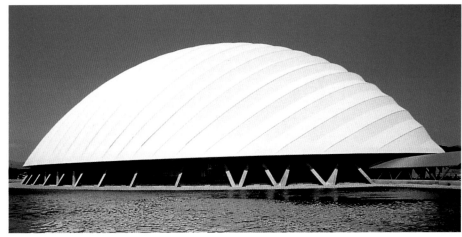

Toyo Ito and Takenaka Corporation

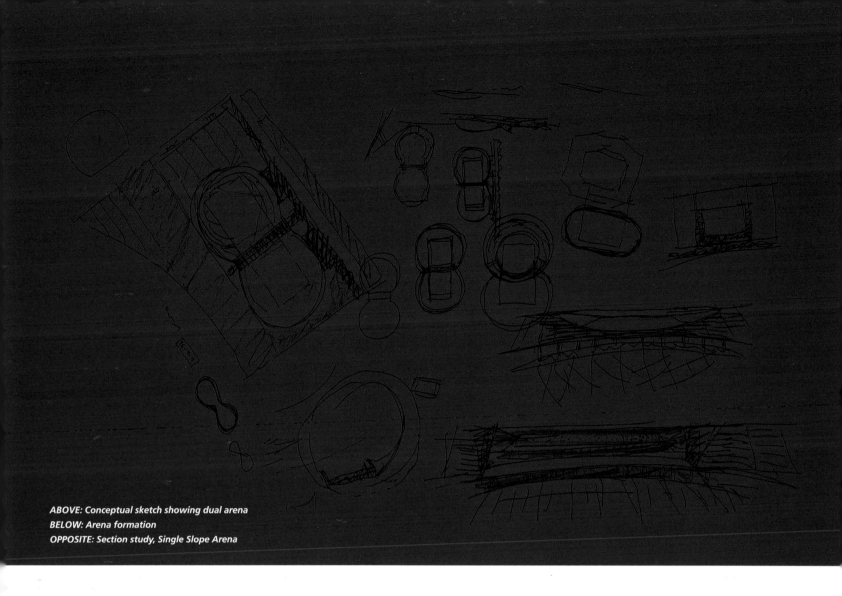

ABOVE: Conceptual sketch showing dual arena
BELOW: Arena formation
OPPOSITE: Section study, Single Slope Arena

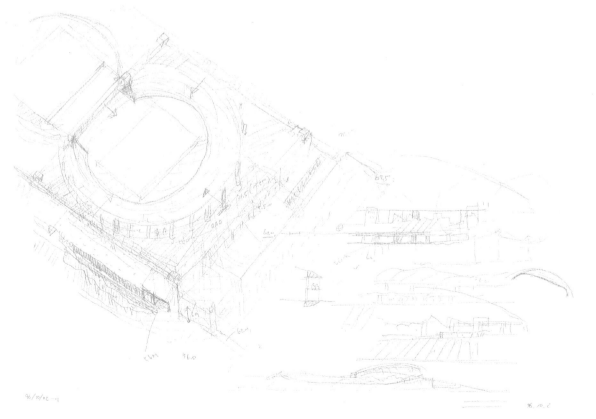

The Hiroshi Hara Group

Hiroshi Hara

Atelier f

Atelier BNK

Takenaka Corporation

Taisei Corporation

Schal Bovis Inc.

Hiroshi Hara

Sapporo Dome

General Design

The cities of Hokkaido have traditionally been designed on an orthogonal grid system imported from overseas. The farmland is divided up in the same way. This unintended coincidence suggests that Japanese culture has links with "gardening" and landscape that affect both urban and rural areas in an integral way.

The Sapporo Dome stands on a finger of farmland penetrating into the urban zone like a pier of nature striding into a sea of artificiality. The compound forms part of the farmland, but at the same time has been fashioned into a "garden of sport." This garden is layered to fit the gently undulating topography of a hill known as Hitsuji-gaoka. There are plans for an urban section of the garden, parallel to the linear urban development along Highway 36. The roof of the dome represents an arbour, while the playing field itself and the surrounding seating suggest the topography. In particular, the turfed soccer field is conceptually a floating or hovering stage designed to cater to a variety of uses.

It was this desire to give the Sapporo Dome the capacity to cater flexibly for many events that led to the concept of a "clopen" (closed-open) spatial structure, where a closed and open environment can be simultaneously experienced or seen in transition. Dome structures built to date can generally be categorized as of a simple type with only a single arena. This proposal is a dome with two arenas. In mathematical terms, it is a complex dome comprising a real, or closed, part and an imaginary, or open, part. The "clopen" structure is based on a dual-arena landscape consisting of a single slope stand arena, designed as gently rolling terrain, and a grass stand arena covered by natural grass. The two aspects of this dual arena are complementary under the "clopen" shell

roof, which is dynamically balanced by a 90m-span bow bridge for a giant opening. The characteristics of the "clopen" space can be altered to suit the function by a variety of mobile systems and movable equipment including a hovering stage.

With its novel dual arena, this dome is expected to attract quality sports events and similar activities, and to inspire those taking part in them. The dual arena and mobile systems will be run by the citizens themselves, with the aim of continuously developing and introducing new landscaping techniques. The beauty of the natural landscape surrounding the dome, and the spacious garden covering a large part of the compound are sure to attract a continuous stream of visitors. The amusement complex will be able to receive these visitors as an extension of the small town, offering constant urban bustle, and a lively streetscape. Even when the facility is closed the dome will remain a dynamic public space or "city in miniature."

The Concept of "Gardening"

A garden is a place where nature and design, body and mind, blend together to represent a culture's ever-changing modality. "Gardening" is a figurative term that we use to contrast with planning to represent the most fundamental design principle on which our proposal is based. Usually, according to contemporary thinking, a range of different events takes place in a planned space. By contrast, we assume in this design that the use of mobile systems and the encouragement of phenomena such as ecosystem growth can, in time, alter the intention of a project. Based on this assumption, we apply the metaphorical term "gardening" to the design of this "sports garden." Through this approach we want to turn the entire compound into a garden,

giving the site the potential to evolve into something better in the future.

Topographical design is the very basis of gardening. An appropriate topographic design should complement the volumes of the existing natural landscape. Here, the geometrical characteristics and boundary conditions of the topography, along with the need for continuity with the surrounding farmland, led us to adopt five zones, named to reflect their function. The botanical zone is a botanical garden covering the embankment along Highway 36. The town zone is the small linear development along the edge of the embankment that connects with the dome. The athletic zone comprises the dual arena and the grass-covered terrace surrounding it. The transportation zone comprises an area of regularly spaced trees among which vehicles pass. The natural zone, irregular in shape, consists of grassland leading up to the surrounding farmland.

Each of these zones exemplifies a different essence of gardening. Each is not a completed ecosystem, but has plenty of potential for future growth into a more stable system. These zones also support the design of the landscape, determining the relationships between the roof of the dome and the other "floating elements." We call the topographical and floating elements that control the appearance of the landscape, such as trees or grassy terraces, "scenery regulators." By adopting the concept of "buoyancy" and floating elements as a basic policy, we give every topographical feature the potential to act as a scenery regulator. The hovering soccer field, covered with natural turf, is a perfect example: this stage actually floats pneumatically when in motion. The arbour-like roof, which hovers above, is the most impressive element, and will dominate all views, floating above the land and soaring into the sky. *HH*

ABOVE: Elevation 1
LEFT: Inner perspective 1

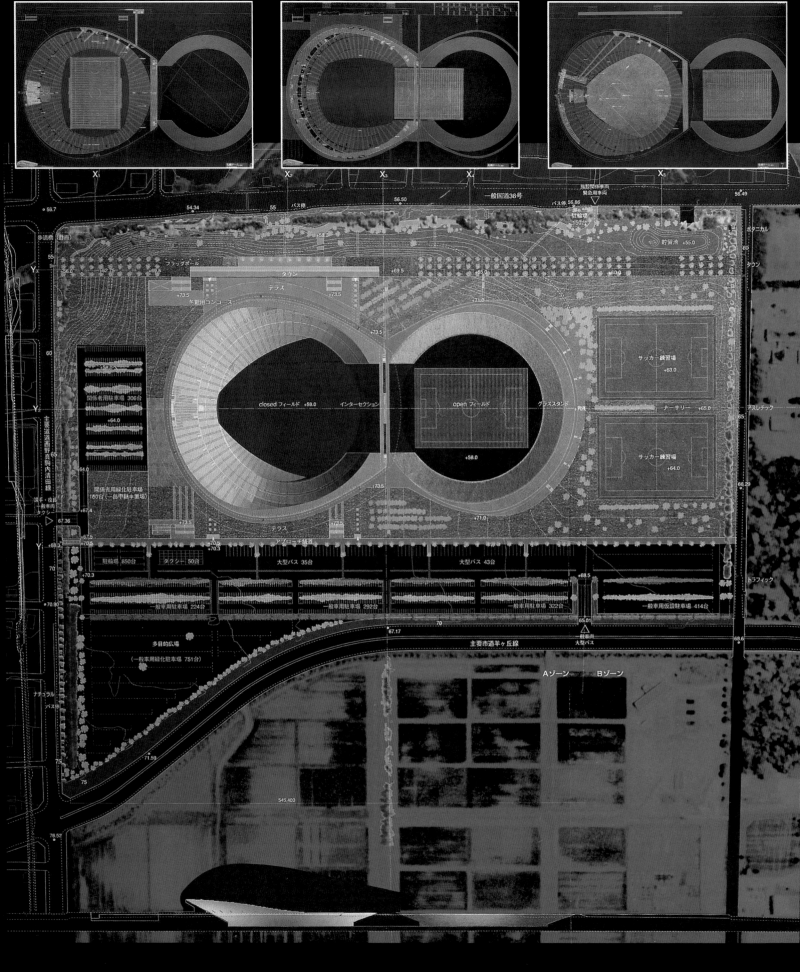

*LEFT: Site plan. TOP LEFT: 4th floor plan with
the movement of the hovering soccer field
TOP CENTRE: 5th floor plan with soccer formation
TOP RIGHT: 6th floor plan with baseball formation
RIGHT TOP: Inner perspective
RIGHT CENTRE: Photo model
RIGHT BOTTOM: Photo model*

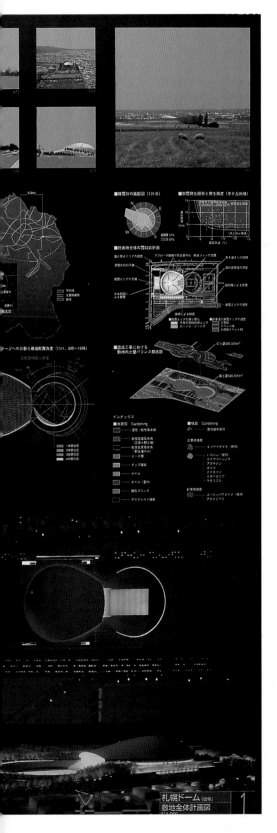

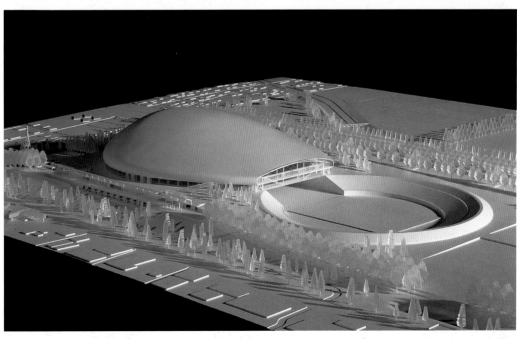

Fumihiko Maki

Makuhari Messe, Phase II

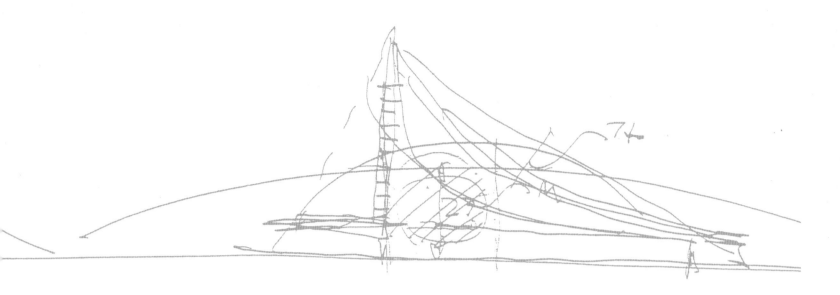

ABOVE: Concept sketch by Maki OPPOSITE: General view from the south-east

The Nippon Convention Centre — more commonly known as the Makuhari Messe — is built on a flat parcel of reclaimed land facing Tokyo Bay, halfway between downtown Tokyo and the International Airport at Narita. The centre was planned as a focus for the newly emerging business and residential centre of Makuhari New Town. We received the commission to design it after winning a national competition in 1986. Combining an exhibition hall, event hall, and international conference centre, the Messe was unprecedented in Japan at that time and was our office's most ambitious project to date. We designed it by allocating the separate parts of the programme into independent buildings of various geometric forms. We located the two relatively smaller buildings — the Event Hall and International Conference Centre — on the north side of the site, forming an informal entrance plaza between them. These buildings, with their pedestrian arcades, exterior stairs and sculptural elements, provide a sense of human scale for visitors approaching the massive complex. The arched silhouette of the gigantic Exhibition Hall roof rises beyond them.

Several years later the Messe was in such intensive use that more halls were needed, and we were selected to design a 33,000 sq.m annex to our earlier complex, to include one large exhibition hall of 9,000 sq.m and additional smaller bays that could be subdivided. A site to the west of the existing Messe was made available. Our first thoughts were to merely extend the length of the existing structure with another arched roof across the street. But after some preliminary studies we discovered that the distance one would have to walk from one end of the exhibition spaces to the other made this impractical.

Instead of predictably enlarging the Exhibition Hall we had by now become interested in using the new building to create a new urban complex made up of complementing parts. We wanted to reflect the passage of time, an idea sprung from our experience in designing projects such as the Hillside Terrace complex and the Iwasaki Museum in distinct phases. An alternative site was chosen north of the existing Event Hall, to lay out the new exhibition halls perpendicular to the original Exhibition Hall. This also strengthened the presence of the outdoor mall, by diverting the flow of people into this landscaped promenade which had been seldom used before.

To complement this outdoor mall, we created an indoor mall which offered dramatic views of the surrounding townscapes. These views remained unobstructed from inside because slender tension bars were chosen instead of roof trusses to support the arched roof. This structure also helped maintain the visual effect of lightness which, in fact, is the leitmotif of the entire second phase.

As in the original Messe, the structural feat of spanning the length of the exhibition hall meant that the roof form had enormous expressive potential. Where the original Messe's arched roof had suggested mountains, for the main exhibition hall of Phase II, we inverted the curve to create a metaphorical wave. This roof uses a hybrid suspension structure, consisting of a series of curved steel trusses suspended from vertical steel poles at 12m intervals. The horizontal forces at the point of suspension are stabilized by backstay cables anchored at the edge of the raised pedestrian deck. The tall poles and tension cables are not mere structure, but inject a festive atmosphere into the Messe, particularly when seen from the approach road.

The roof of the large exhibition hall is formed as a catenary curve — structurally the

Location:
Makase, Makuhari New Town, Chiba Prefecture

Site area:
43,960 sq.m

Building area:
30,572 sq.m

Total floor area:
33,413 sq.m

Structural system:
SRC and steel (roof structure),
2 storeys and tower

Structural engineer:
SDG

Mechanical/electrical engineer:
Sogo Consultants

Landscape consultant:
Equipe Espace

Contractor:
Joint venture with Shimizu, Ohayashi, Mitsui

Completion date:
September 1997

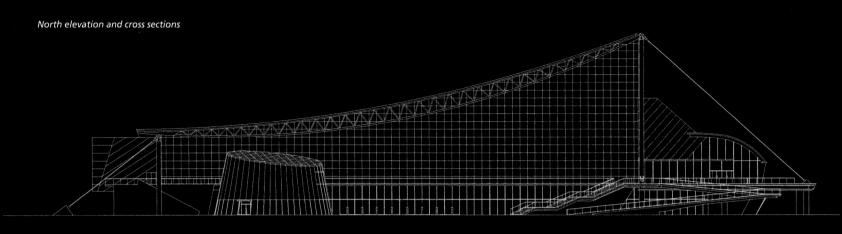

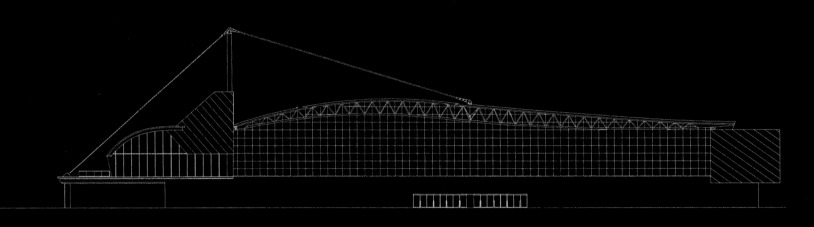

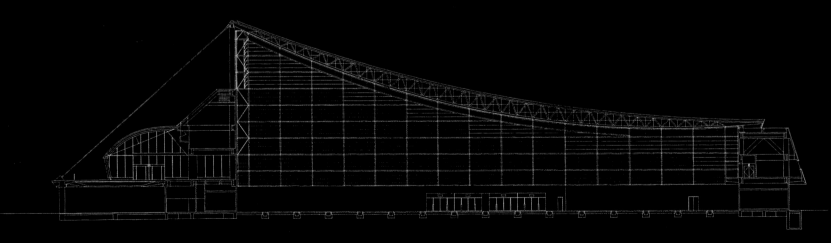

most efficient shape for a roof load in tension — and rises to a height of 32m. Clerestory windows around its periphery dramatize the lightness of its structure. The roof of the two adjacent halls has a more complex wave-like curve that turns downward at the east end, to contrast with the catenary curve.

The sequential organization of the halls and public spaces is similar to that of the original Messe, which had proved a success. Entrances to the exhibitions are located on a raised pedestrian deck, so that visitors can see the whole exhibition space at a glance before descending to the main floor. An entrance plaza featuring an elliptical conference room pavilion is located at the south end of the site, diagonally across from the larger plaza of the original Messe. Protected by the roof's giant curved trusses, this space provides an outdoor public place where large events take place. *FM*

ABOVE: The new second phase seen together with the first phase BELOW: Site plan

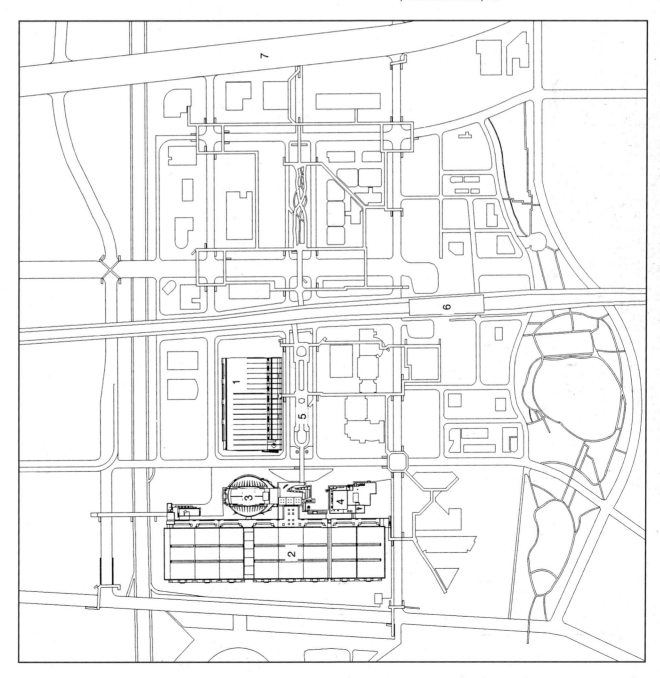

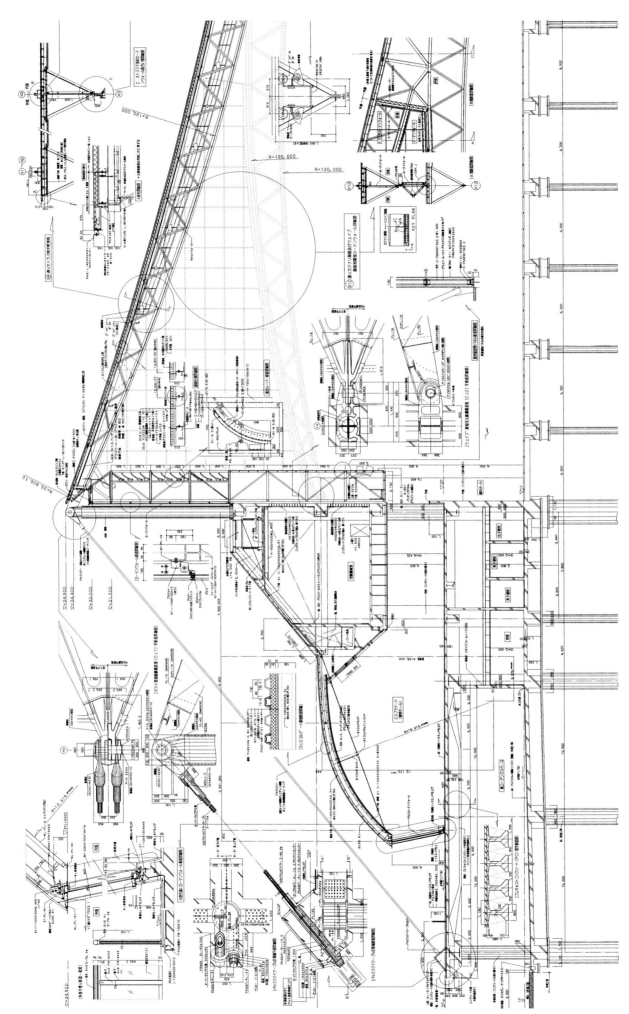

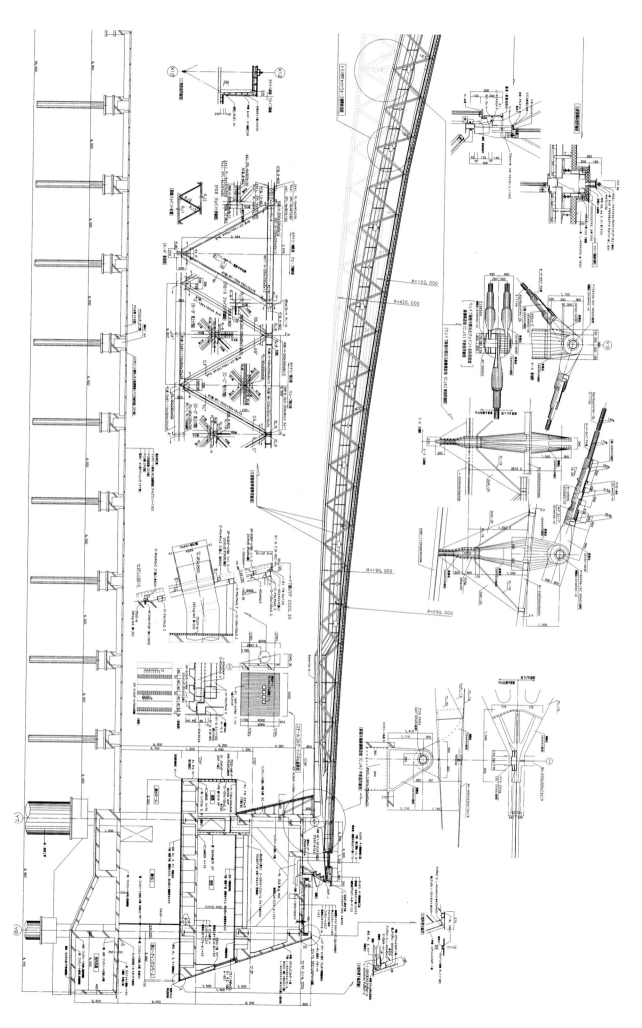

Location:
Sakyo, Kyoto, Japan

Design:
Tadao Ando

Site area:
2824 m²

Building area:
28 m²

Total floor area:
212.2 m²

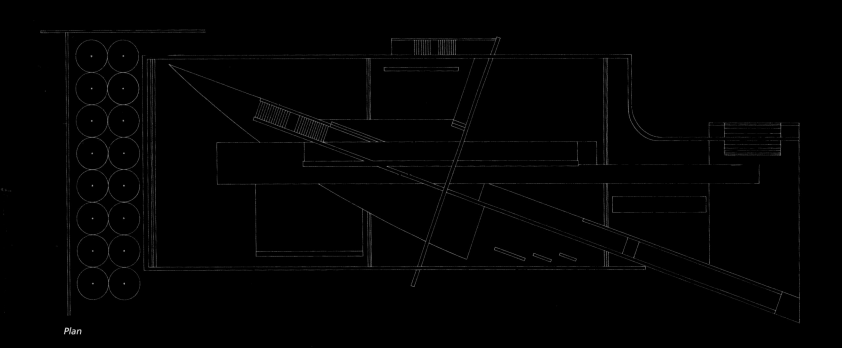

Plan

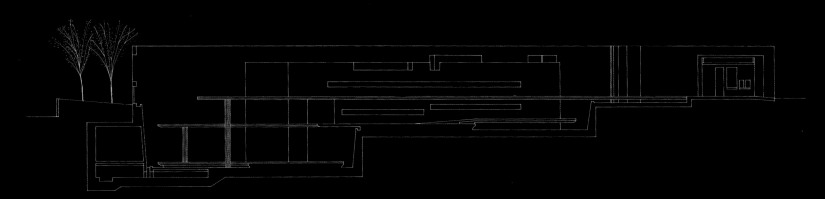

Section

Tadao Ando

Garden of Fine Arts, Kyoto

Layered facets of light and shadow

LEFT: View from the south towards the entrance
on the right
ABOVE: View from the entrance looking south
RIGHT TOP: Lowest B2 level looking south
RIGHT MIDDLE: View of the upper, street level
with pool, seen from the entrance
RIGHT BOTTOM: Lowest B2 level looking east

The Garden of Fine Arts is located next to a botanical garden on Kitayama Boulevard and is an outdoor museum for the enjoyment of masterpieces of Western and Japanese art while in contact with natural phenomena such as light, wind and water. The museum itself is a conceptual extension of Ando's Garden of Fine Arts in Osaka designed for the 1990 Garden and Greenery Exposition (1988-90), and reflects his long interest in developing processional spaces along the approaches to such projects as the Water Temple (1989-91) and the Church on the Water (1985-88). Here, such outdoor spatial sequences constitute the entire project.

An enclosed sunken area is designed below ground level within which three walls and circulation, consisting of bridges and ramps, create a rich variety of spaces on three levels. Water is introduced into the experience through three waterfalls and pools at each level.

The project was conceived as a contemporary, volumetric version of a traditional stroll garden.

Location: 215 Taisho-cho,
Sakaiminato-shi, Tottori Prefecture
Function:
Ferry terminal, public baths,
community hall
Levels: 4 storeys
Structure: Reinforced concrete
with steel frame
Site area: 5,080.30 sq.m
Building area: 1,993.73 sq.m
Total floor area: 4,049.92 sq.m
Structural Engineers: Dan Structure Design
Mechanical Engineers:
Architectural Environmental Laboratory
General Contractor:
JV of Toda Corporation,
Akagi Construction and Miho Doken

The city of Sakaiminato was historically the most important trading port with Russia, China and Korea and still is today. To encourage interaction among diverse visitors, the centre was designed to house a ferry terminal, public baths, exhibition spaces, and offices for various port associations. Yet it was also required to be a symbol for the centre of Japanese maritime communication with the rest of the world. Four cylinders and a curved wall radically achieve this by symbolising a wave with transport ships on top.

Shin Takamatsu

+ Shin Takamatsu Architect & Associates

Ashdod Cultural Hall
Ashdod, Israel
Concert Hall
Reinforced concrete with steel frame

Osaka Port Ferry Terminal Complex
Shin Takamatsu and Shin Takamatsu Architects & Associates

Location: Konohana-ku, Osaka-shi, Osaka
Function: Ferry Terminal, Hotel, Commercial, Cultural
Levels: 2 basements and 16 storeys
Structure: Steel frame and reinforced concrete
Site area: 8,600 sq.m
Building area: 4,324 sq.m
Total floor area: 42,980 sq.m

The site is located in an area of great development in Osaka Bay, home to the Asia-Pacific Trade Centre, the World Trade Centre, the Suntory Museum and Universal Studios, Japan, which is under construction. All these seem to make up what looks like a huge fleet, although one without a flagship. To unite and compose these ships to look outwards towards the world a flagship was required. And so this project was named the Flagship Project. It consists of a shopping area, in the form of waves like the sea, with a hotel high above like a luxury ship sailing the sea. The sea and the ship work in harmony.

Hamada Children's Museum of Art

Location: Shimane Prefecture
Function: Museum, workshop
Levels: 5 storeys
Structure: Reinforced concrete

Earthtecture Sub-1, Shibuya-ku, Tokyo
Function: Retail
Levels: 4 basements
Structure: Reinforced concrete
Site area: 172.48 sq.m
Building area: 60.96 sq.m
Total floor area: 455.10 sq.m
Structural engineers: Yamamoto-Tachibana Architects & Engineers
Mechanical Engineers: Architectural Environmental Laboratory
General Contractor: Konoike Construction

A computer company and information library. These butterfly-shaped toplights bring natural light to underground levels.

Misumi Public Elementary School
Location: Mishumi-cho, Naka-gun, Shimane Prefecture
Function: Elementary School
Levels: 2 storeys
Structure: Reinforced concrete and steel frame
Site area: 42,592.54 sq.m
Building area: 5,812.94 sq.m
Total floor area: 7,837.83 sq.m
Structural Engineers: Dan Structure Design
Mechanical Engineers: Architectural Environmental Laboratory
General Contractor: JV of Goyo Construction and Miyata Construction Ltd.
Design: September 1994-October 1995
Construction : October 1995-March 1997

This small public elementary school for 412 students consists of two circles of different sizes; the inner circle has a garden in the centre. The corridor along the inner garden is an atrium full of natural light, leading to the classrooms. The classroom wall facing the corridor is removable so that the children can enjoy natural scenery integrated into their classroom. The simple geometric composition produces flexible spaces. Specific rooms, such as the workshop, library, and music room, are placed at random around water features in the inner garden. Thus the water element and the children's lives are woven into the space, providing protection from the strong seasonal wind yet allowing them to breathe in the richness of the wind.

Shikatsu Town Welfare Centre
Ooaze, Kumanoshou,
Aichi Prefecture
Centre for senior citizens, the
handicapped, and the local community
Steel frame with reinforced concrete

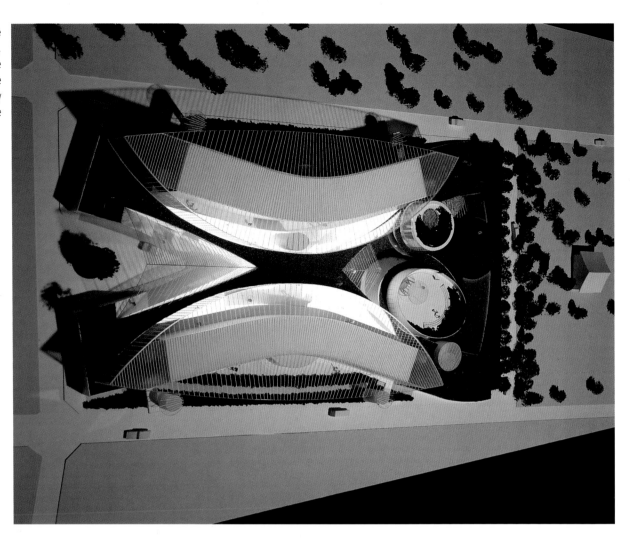

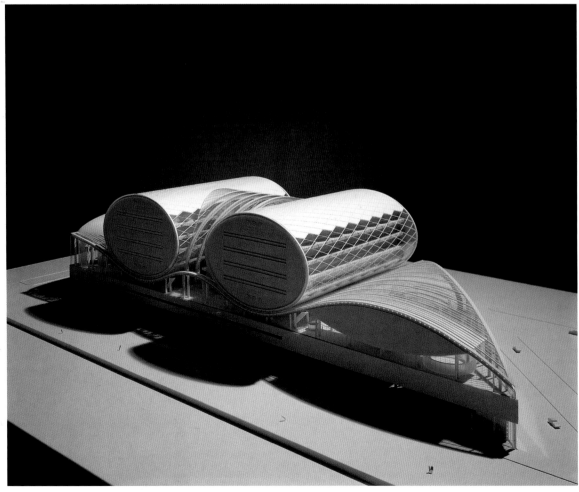

UCSF Campus Proposal
Mission Bay, San Francisco, CA, USA
UCSF school campus
(Bio-Medical Laboratory)
Steel with reinforced concrete

Ela Tower
Tel Aviv, Israel
Office, Hotel
Steel frame

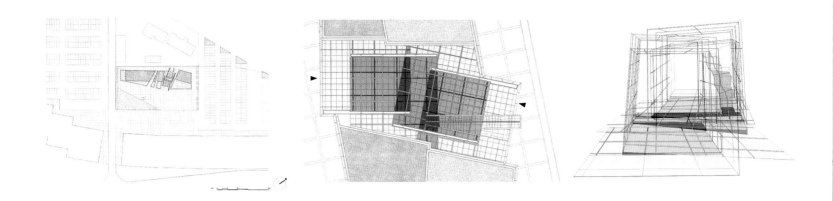

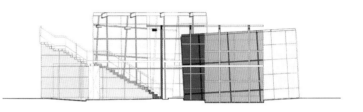

Hiromi Fujii

Folly in Matto City and Passage in the Park

ABOVE: West elevation
BELOW: Interior view from the north
OPPOSITE TOP (from left to right): Site plan, plan, diagram
MIDDLE: Section
BOTTOM: View towards the staircase

This folly is located in a suburb of Matto, a municipality approximately halfway between Kanazawa, the main city in the Hokuriku region facing the Sea of Japan, and Komatsu. Matto is a provincial city of about 30,000 inhabitants. It has long benefited from its position in a fertile farming belt and has continued to develop in more recent times by attracting large enterprises to the area. During the past few years, the city has initiated plans to build a new city hall and to develop the central district and some peripheral districts.

At present, the peripheral districts being developed are mainly in the area facing the Sea of Japan. Leisure facilities, a power plant using natural energy, spas and indoor pools are being built along the Hokuriku Expressway, which follows the coastline.

The folly was only one of many projects and the development of the area into a leisure-oriented district with large commercial facilities, hotels, a concert hall, parks and a man-made island is expected over the next two or three years.

At first, the project was conceived as a functionless folly standing in a plaza in the commercial facilities zone. However, as it developed, increased awareness of the boundary with other sites led to a demand for a connection that transcended the boundary between other sites and the plaza. Ultimately, the goal became the creation of a passage space offering a view rather than a folly. The passage lies on the boundary between a zone where commercial facilities will be constructed and a parking area belonging to another group. The boundary consists of a belt of plants, some of which were cleared to make way for the passage.

And yet the passage does not have to be in that specific place. In this sense, the project retains its original character as a folly.

Local people call the passage "the undulating road." This is because the floor surfaces appear to tilt like waves.

The space is composed of four types of rectangular spatial units. These units overlap, leaning forwards and backwards and to the left and to the right, and traverse the boundary as if they are carving their way through it. The reds and greens in the spaces and the grey gridded joints enable observers to decode the spatial organization but they are not intended to serve solely as decoding media.

The tilting and overlapping of floor, wall and ceiling surfaces and the criss-crossing of gridded joints on these surfaces do not promote decoding so much as generate a sense of divergence and ambiguity. This sense of ambiguous divergence reveals not an ordinary scene but an unfamiliar scene that is simply a composition. This scene, which is designed simply to be looked at, I call scenery, but it could also be called reality. As people pass through the space, the floor surface, which tilts at a right angle to the wall surface, provides a body touching it directly with a stimulus that is like an undulation. Like a sonic stimulus, this stimulus generates an immediate sense inside the body, an internal sense. This internal sense, eventually superseded by scenery or reality, gives rise to diverse events.

This passage is designed as a prototype for a passage-cum-windscreen for this coastal district, where there are strong winds. Eventually it will no doubt criss-cross the coastal district and generate diverse events. *HF*

RIGHT: Detail of ceiling
BELOW: Staircase

ABOVE: View from sightseeing space, staircase and floor
LEFT: View from the north

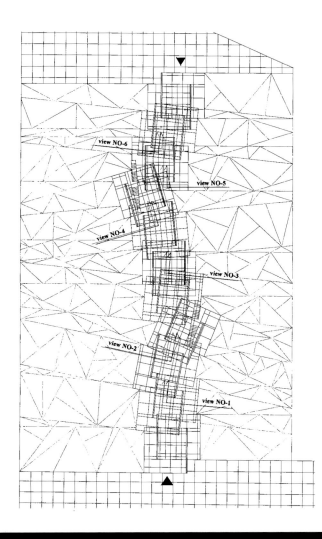

Passage in the park

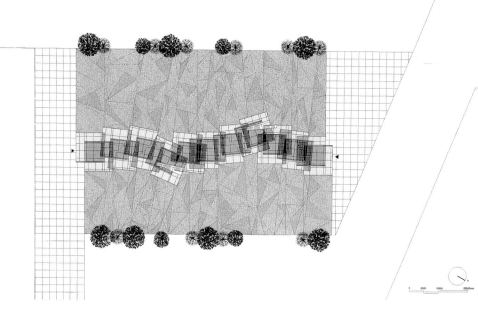

LEFT: View from each place
ABOVE: Plan
BELOW LEFT: View NO-1
BELOW RIGHT: View NO-3

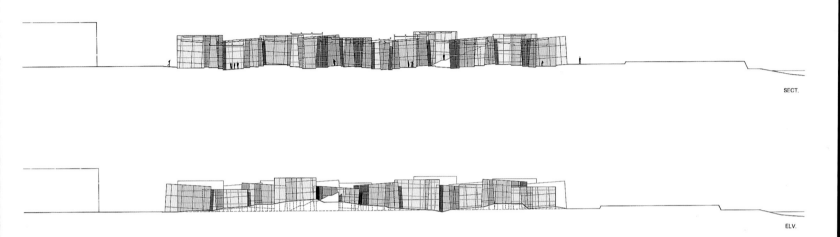

SECT.

ELV.

ABOVE: Section and elevation
BELOW LEFT: View NO-4
BELOW RIGHT: View NO-5

The aim of the project was to consolidate three existing municipal high schools into an entirely new school, equipped with not only a new building but also a new educational program. The competition brief made it clear that this was not to be a traditional school based on home rooms, but a school with classrooms dedicated to different subjects of the curriculum. The mayor of Iwedeyama was eager for it to be an innovative project. The new buildings were to do nothing less than to revitalize a town experiencing depopulation, and translate this town's slogan - "community development through learning" - into reality. Many hopes were resting on the project.

For curriculum and spatial organisation there were to be four subject areas–language, mathematics and science, domestic science, and art. Each subject area was to be provided with its special classrooms, such as laboratories, audiovisual rooms and libraries, research rooms for the teachers, and a media gallery (a room for accessing information and material). Each area would be independent, although, ultimately, it was up to each architect to propose the inter-relationships between subject area and physical space. The competition left a great deal up to the architect.

We proposed composing the school in two domains: classrooms for courses in the curricula organized around the media gallery, and an area for everyday student life organized around the student lounges. The media gallery is a place for information and material related to subject courses and also a work room for teachers and students. The media gallery and adjoining classrooms can be joined together and freely adapted to different uses.

The locker rooms and the multi-purpose hall we combined to create places for the students' everyday communal life, separated from the teaching areas. The locker rooms became "student lounges", and the multi-purpose hall became the "student forum". These eighteen student lounges float above the forum. They were integrated in a huge atrium, topped by an enormous roof. This atrium, at the centre of the school, is the main circulation and gathering space. Our view was to encourage this communal life. A school is not just a place for education. The teachers' research rooms, located below the student forum, are not really faculty rooms, nor places for student guidance, but spaces in which teachers can conduct research in their specialised fields. There are three research rooms - one for the Japanese and English teachers in the language curriculum, a second for the mathematics and science teachers in the natural science curriculum, and a third for the teachers in the domestic science curriculum.

The competition brief stressed that this was also to be a facility for the people of the town. In ten years, it is expected that the student enrolment should be half what it is now, so that the building could function as a cultural and sports facility for the town's citizens too. Our proposal was to arrange various spaces - a music room, an art room, a computer room, a language laboratory, and a metal and wood workshop - around a plaza open to the townspeople to be called the "forest plaza". The building is designed to accommodate a gradual shift in its role as the student enrolment shrinks.

Riken Yamamoto

Iwadeyama Junior High School, Iwadeyama

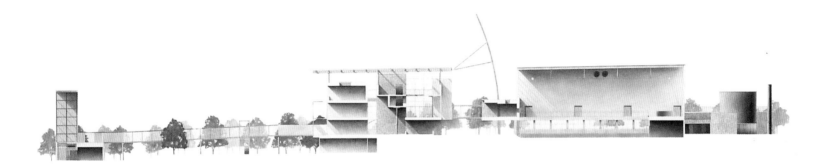

ABOVE: Elevation
BELOW: Distant view of the School from the adjacent sports field

Interior views

These various functional areas are arranged in strips that form a series extending north and south. Each strip has its own role, although each interrelates. Transparent materials are used freely to make these interrelationships visible from any vantage point, and in practice to make it possible to look from one strip into another, and ahead into another. For instance, standing in the student forum, one can see classes in progress, the faculty center in full swing and the inside of the gymnasium. Standing in the media gallery, one can see the research rooms, and beyond them the "arcade of light" (a place for accessing points of vertical circulation); the student forum is visible overhead, and turning around, one can spy the classrooms through openings provided in fixtures. It is not a case of one side supervising the other side; instead, people on different sides are able to see and communicate with one another. One can see not only the adjacent strip but the strip beyond it.

The "wing of the wind" is a wall protecting the school from the north wind in winter and a reflective panel for introducing additional light. This wall also made construction work considerably easier. However, we were most interested in the visual impact it would have when seen from the Rikuu Higashi railway line and National Road Number 7, below the hill. This hilltop had been selected as the site of the school precisely because of its symbolic prominence. The competition brief included a comment that "a mountaintop with a view of the earth below possesses not only a prospect but the power to induce large-mindedness." This was a place waiting for a symbol. It now has one.

Masaharu Takasaki

Kihoku Astronomical Museum

Location: Uwaba Park, 1660-3 Ichinari, Kihoku-cho, Kagoshima-ken
Principal Use: Astronomical Observatory, Museum and Community Centre
Completion: July, 1995
Structural Engineers: Tanaka Institute, Waseda University
Site Area: 5,287.97 sq m
Building Area: 425.54 sq m
Total Floor Area: 427.6 sq m
Structure: reinforced concrete, 4 storeys

Kihoku Astronomical Museum is in Kihoku-cho, a town of approximately 4,800 inhabitants. The town is currently experiencing problems because of the exodus of large numbers of its younger citizen, leaving behind an aging population. But the natural environment of the town remains very beautiful: it is located in the hills and for four years now has won the Environment Agency award for the most stunning night skies in Japan in summer and winter. The essential theme of this project was to enliven the town using the theme of beautiful night skies.

Architecture lives with its chosen site. When new architecture is sited in a local environment, I have to study the history, society, culture and topography of the area. I always start my projects by trying to communicate with the chosen site. The museum here is located in the Kihoku Uwaba Park at a height of 550m, with views of Sakurajima, an active volcano, and Kinko Bay to the west, Miyakonojo Basin to the east, the Kirishima mountain range to the north, and Shibushi Bay to the south. Such beautiful scenery captivated me. It was clearly the perfect place for the museum. But I also try to work with the global environment, to stimulate it, and to analyze theoretically all the factors affecting the chosen site from a wider perspective, to find a symbolic geometry that communicates with the land organically.

While this more scientific approach is true, producing architecture often comes from a vaguer, more unconscious relatyionship to the environment. I intended to place myself as an invisible presence in the spirit of the town. From this the Kihoku Astronomical Museum would grow as an abstract form derived from the history, nature, society and culture of Kihoku-cho. It was the spirit of Kihoku-cho that led to the creation of an astronomical architecture facility symbolizing communication with space.

Visiting Taskasaki's fascinating architecture in and around Kagoshima, particularly his Tamana City Observatory Museum and Kihoku Astronomical Observatory and Museum, is, to say the least, a rare experience. Nowadays, one seldom comes across an architect with such a powerful imagination and ability, nor with such a strong commitment to conjuring up unexpected, long forgotten, and yet uniquely new worlds in our age of efficiency, rationalism, and spiritual deprivation.

It is as if natural and atavistic forces are tamed and shaped through the hands of a magician. Takasaki's designs radiate such a magnetic dynamism, that even the most sceptical would be held captive by their irresistible power. Sometimes "tortured", fragmented and scattered, the apparently chaotic forms of his creations, buildings, structures, and models alike, are like animated biomorphic organisms, working together in a mysterious way. They prove that the rational is merely one among the orders that guide human life.

Experiencing the magical world of Takasaki's architecture, one is overcome by a tremendous awe, the kind of awe experienced when looking at images taken by the Hubbell telescope, images which tell of the unimaginable depths of the universe. It is the experience of coming face to face with the infinity and timelessness of the cosmos, the inexplicable and the unexplainable, the dimensions of the unknown.

Growing from the earth and reaching to the skies, Takasaki's works are messengers between micro- and macrocosms, the terrestrial and the celestial, as well as past and future, and science and mythology or imagination. They also act as both a curious telescope and a magic mirror in which we as humans can catch a rare glimpse not only of the mysteries of the universe, but also of ourselves.

Botond Bognar

Remote view with Kagoshima Bay in the background

LEFT: Detail of stairway to the entrance with detail of upper terrace
OPPOSITE: General view of the complex

LEFT: View from the upper terrace and courtyard
BELOW: View from lower court garden with the ramp and the fountain/pool designed by Peter Walker

Yoshio Taniguchi

Toyota Municipal Museum of Art, Toyota City

This museum, one of Taniguchi's latest and largest works, is located in Toyota, where the famous Japanese car maker has its headquarters and main factories. The city, which has seen tremendous progress since the Company started its operations there, was in the Edo Period (1603-1868) a small castle town called Koromo. The museum is located near the former site of the castle, which has been partially reconstructed. The location is a typical castle site on top of a high hill with commanding views of both the castle ruins and the far-spreading new and booming city, establishing in this way a subtle link between past and present.

Owing to the sloping site conditions, the museum has been designed as a three-dimensional spatial matrix with approaches on several levels. Open public plazas on both the first and second levels are connected by a ramp and a stairway on the west side of the complex. Visitors coming from the railway station approach the site from the east and arrive at the second level, where they first enter into a small, separate gallery. This gallery is dedicated to the work of Setsuro Takahashi, a famous lacquer artist and is linked to the main volume of the museum on the lower levels, while on the second level a long canopy, which stretches along the entrance court and sculpture garden of the gallery, and a large terrace are located on top of part of the lower levels. The passage under the canopy looks out over an artificial pond on the west side.

The entrance to the Museum is on the first level and so visitors coming from the second level terrace have to use the stairway leading to the partially enclosed lower entrance plaza, in effect a "sunken" court, which is directly accessible to those coming by car who approach the museum from the west. The first floor accommodates the entrance hall, some small galleries, a lecture hall, a reading room, and the museum shop; administration, the service entrance, and storage area are on the floor below. The second and third floors feature the exhibition galleries, in addition to a restaurant, which is located on the second floor facing the large terrace.

This main part of the Museum is enclosed in a white glazed rectangular volume, while the Takahashi Gallery, the long canopy, and the lower levels are defined by solid walls clad in green stone. The attractive use of special materials, fine detailing and craftsmanship, as well as spatial variety give a sophisticated character to Taniguchi's otherwise crisp and straightforward design, which reaches its climax in the series of galleries softly lit through large frosted glass surfaces.

The equally outstanding site planning and garden design were the work of the American lanscape designer, Peter Walker, with whom Taniguchi had already collaborated on several projects.

Botond Bognar

ABOVE: The volume of the main galleries seen from the
upper terrace with the long canopy
BELOW: Interior detail
OPPOSITE TOP: View of the two courtyards on the
upper terrace
OPPOSITE BOTTOM: Upper terrace with two canopies
over the main approach and entrance
 84 and 85: Upper lobby of main gallery

Featured Projects

ABOVE: General view
LEFT: Inner courtyard with Aiko Miyawaki's sculpture
RIGHT: Composition study.

Arata Isozaki & Associates

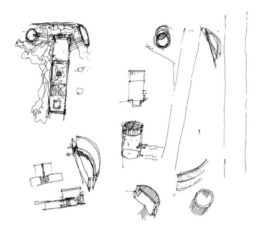

Nagi Museum of Contemporary Art, Nagi

The Nagi Museum of Contemporary Art is an entirely new type of contemporary art museum. The museum as a building type has been undergoing an evolution ever since the nineteenth century, both in content and in form. Nagi-MOCA is what might be called a third-generation art museum.

What makes this museum even more noteworthy is its location. Local governments all over Japan have been rushing to construct cultural facilities – too often simple boxes put up without much forethought – but it is the virtually unknown town of Nagi in Okayama Prefecture which has given birth to the unique project presented here.

Nagi MOCA may well be the first attempt of its kind in the international art world and it will no doubt provide a model for architectural spaces that are adapted to the art of today and of the future.

Art Museums came into being at the beginning of the nineteenth century as places to exhibit royal and aristocratic collections. Works of art from ancient times onward were collected and exhibited, the paintings framed and the sculptures placed on pedestals. The art works were in many cases torn from their original settings to be brought together under one roof. The Louvre and the Tokyo National Museum are examples of first-generation art museums. Modern art, beginning with Impressionism, emerged in the late nineteenth century in opposition to the authority of such museums. The movement called modernism ultimately reduced art works to planes and solid geometrical figures. Art museums with adjustable floors and walls were considered ideal for exhibiting such works. The Pompidou Centre, the New York Museum of Modern Art and many of the so-called museums of modern art in Japan are examples of second-generation art museums.

Since the 1960s, contemporary artists have continued to experiment, conceiving works that transcend the materiality of planes and solids and extend to the spaces (or rooms) in which those planes and solids are arranged. Art museums that exhibit such works have not existed hitherto.

A museum of this kind involves the architecturalization of spaces conceived by living artists. We are witnessing in fragmentary form the begin-ning of a trend towards third-generation art museums in the so-called museums of con-temporary art.

At Nagi-MOCA, three artists – Shusaku Arakawa, Kazuo Okazaki and Aiko Miyawaki – have been asked to conceive works that cannot be accommodated in conventional museum galleries.

The spaces for these works have been integrated into the architecture. Each work is intended to be entered and experienced physically, but it also possesses a configuration that can be clearly recognized from the outside. The sun, the moon and the earth are used as metaphors in all three works (or places).

Each work will be created in situ. That is, it will be site specific. Since it will assimilate every element of the interior space (including configuration, light, materials, viewpoints and time), an observer must visit the site and enter and experience the work to appreciate it. It is hoped that the observer will mediate on the work using all his senses. Media such as photography, print or video can never completely communicate its spatial aura.

The collaboration of architects and artists in this way for the production of spatial works will be the only way of collecting and exhibiting works of art in the future.

What makes Nagi-MOCA especially important is that this approach is being taken by a public museum.

Structural Consultants:
Toshio Yanagisawa Engineering Office
Mechanical Consultants:
Kankyo Engineering Inc.
Lighting Consultants:
TL Yamagiwa Laboratory Inc.
Furniture Consultants:
Fujie Kazuko Atelier Co. Ltd
Signage Consultants:
Ikko Tanaka Design Studio
Staff:
Shuichi Fujie, Ko Ono, Hiroyuki Fukuyama, Kuniaki Takahashi, Luo Ruiyang, Shiyo Shinohara
General Contractor:
Taisai Corporation
Site Area:
7072 sq.m
Building Area:
1545.03 sq.m
Total Floor Area:
1887.21 sq.m

THIS PAGE
RIGHT TOP: North elevation; RIGHT BOTTOM:
South elevation; MIDDLE: East elevation; BOTTOM
LEFT:Site plan; BOTTOM RIGHT: Roof plan
OPPOSITE
TOP LEFT: Second floor plan; TOP RIGHT: First
floor plan; MIDDLE: Perspective;
BOTTOM: Isometrics

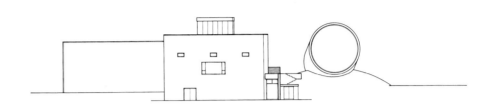

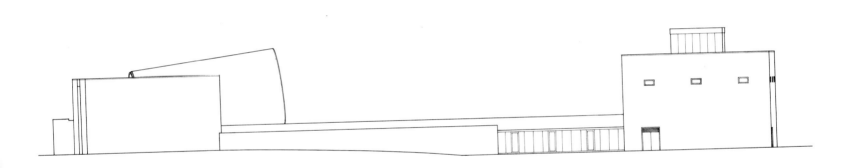

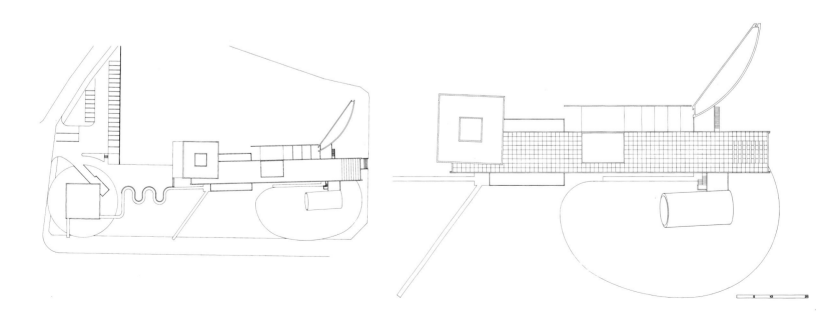

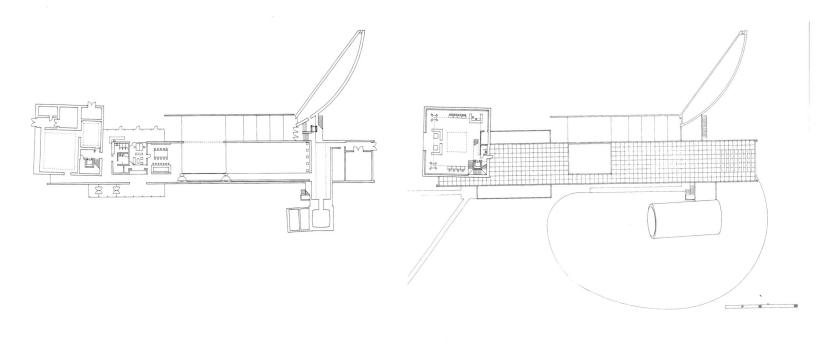

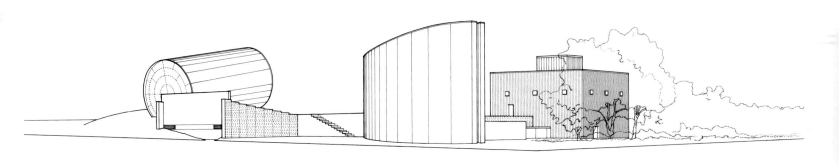

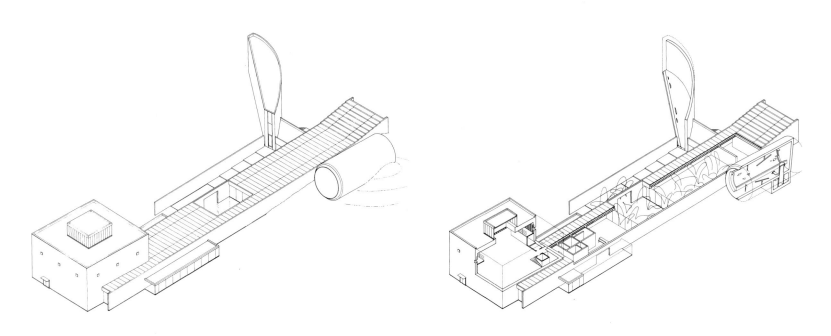

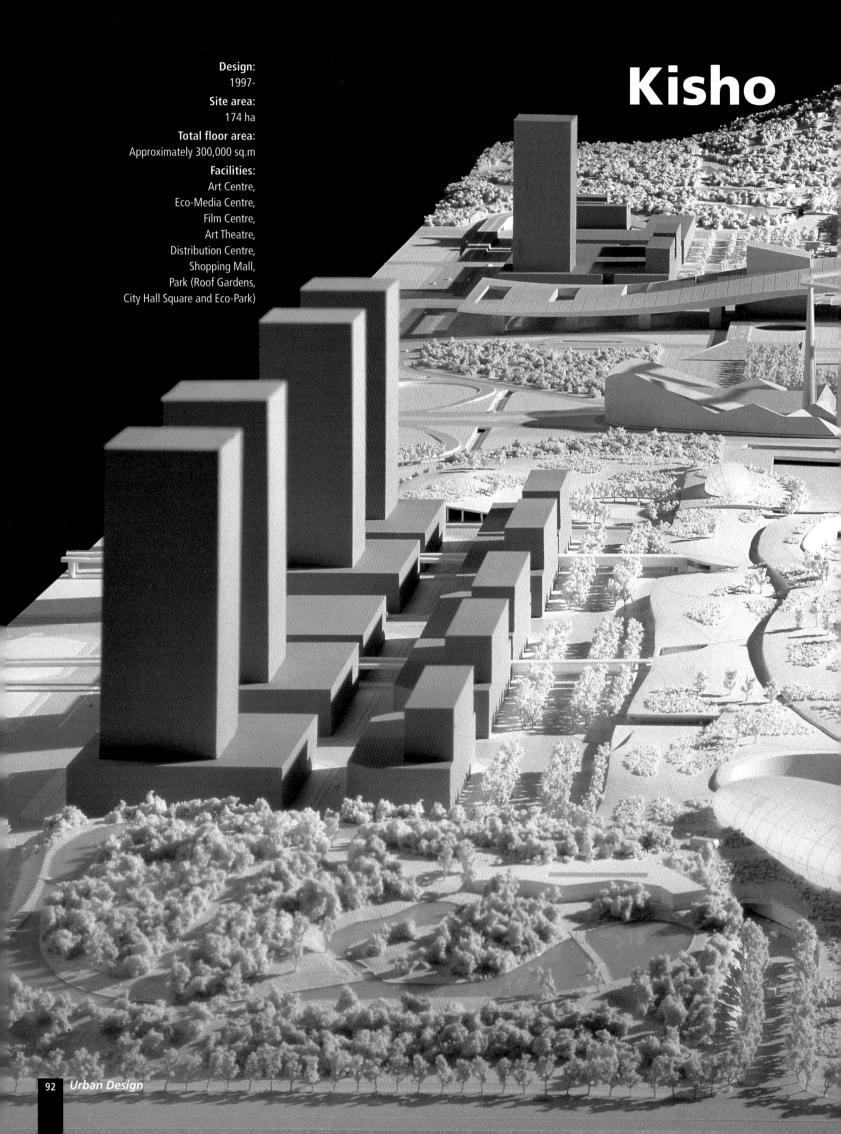

Design:
1997-

Site area:
174 ha

Total floor area:
Approximately 300,000 sq.m

Facilities:
Art Centre,
Eco-Media Centre,
Film Centre,
Art Theatre,
Distribution Centre,
Shopping Mall,
Park (Roof Gardens,
City Hall Square and Eco-Park)

Kisho

Kurokawa

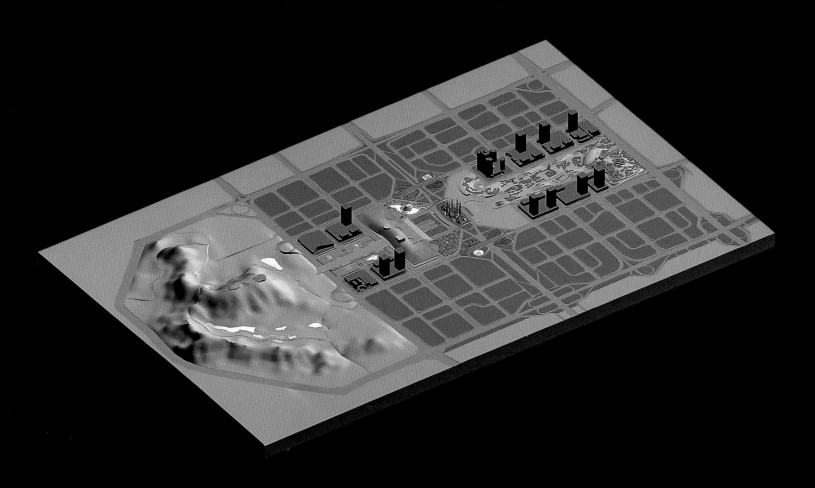

PREVIOUS PAGES: Model
ABOVE: Perspective
BELOW: Location

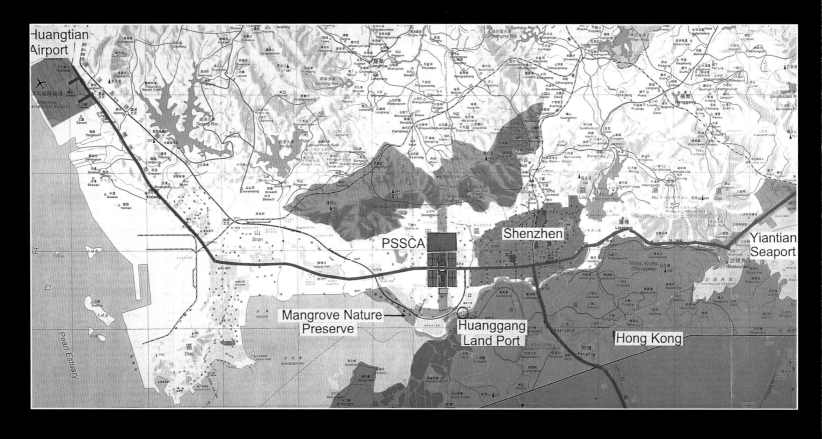

Urban Design

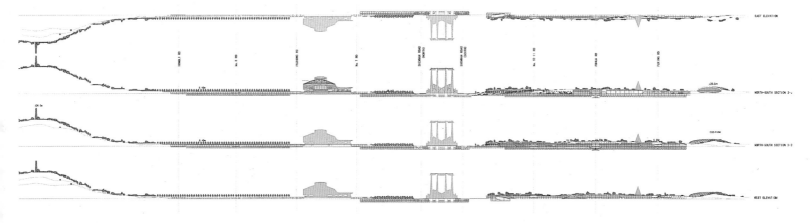

Sections

OVERALL CONCEPT

This project is based on Kisho Kurokawa's Eco-Media City Project Plan. In the city centre of Shenzhen SEZ (Special Economic Zone) adjacent to Hong Kong, an open space of 3km in length will be planned with the new city hall (the design of which is to be the subject of an international competition) at its centre.

At both ends of the site, parks making the best use of the natural environment will be provided, and in between them, a park will be built on man-made subsoil. Underneath the subsoil, many facilities such as an Art Centre will be provided, and its aim is to become a new Mecca for artistic events, such as the biennale and the triennale. The Public Space System of the Central Axis (PSSCA) will not be just a park system but an Eco-Media City Park providing infrastructure that will generate many urban and multi-media industrial activities for the economy, such as distribution centres, a business incubation centre and an information hub.

The design concept is taken from the method of music composition using an "urban score."

LOCATION

The PSSCA is well located to become an eco-media hub for Shenzhen. It is linked via Shennan road to both Huangtian Airport and the existing downtown area, making it an important part of a growing information corridor running east to west. By designing according to the principles of symbiosis, the co-existence of both ecological park areas and eco-technology and media-technology can be achieved together.

The green axis of the PSSCA is also easily linked to the land port of Huanggang and the

nature reserve area of Mangrove Jungle. Thus, a green corridor running from north to south is established from the PSSCA's Lianhua Mountain to the sea. The green belt along the river also connects the PSSCA with Old Shenzhen.

3-D SPACE PLANNING

Conventional city planning creates land-use zones on a two-dimensional plane. But this proposal for will also arrange land-use three-dimensionally in layers as an "urban score," with the symbiotic use of a park on the roof-tops and pedestrian sky bridge links to city community centre. This should create an integrated and symbiotic urban fabric with commerce that will not decline and spaces that will come to life in the evening.

In the Basement, the first layer includes a shopping park and mall with parking and subway access. Above this the Ground Level, layer two, is made up of city offices, a science museum, an art museum and art park, a "media incubation centre," a bus station, shopping mall and distribution centre. These functions extend onto the Second Floor, layer three, which also houses the Tree-shaded Park and the Ceremonial Park. On the Third Floor, layer four, the Traditional Park, Symbiotic Roof Garden, Eco-Park and Eco-Media Offices are planned.

THE URBAN SCORE: CONCEPT

A musical score provides the information that enables a number of musicians to play together in harmony. The composition as a whole is a multi-layered complex interrelation of notes and rhythms which depend as much upon the space between (the rests) as on the notes themselves. Likewise the Urban Score approaches urban design as a series of

layers: Time Sequence, Movement, Function, Event, Morphology, Metaphor and Vista. As in music the spaces and relationships between the elements are intrinsic and the complete design a rich, complex multi-dimensional experience.

Time Sequence

Stave 1 of the composition of Shenzhen speaks of the transition and sequence of time through the site. Moving from Lianhua Hill to the Eco-Park to the south this concept is realized by the planting and subsequent blooming of seasonal flowers through the site. As the time changes the flowers in bloom will migrate south, making each season a celebration, and each part of the site a place to celebrate. As the space between the notes is important so the transition between the seasons is of special importance. For instance, Lianhua Hill will host the celebration of spring in its natural environment. Perstylus Spiranthes, Moralda, and Jigitaris bloom in spring and represent the beginning of life.

Morphology

The dynamics of music is created by the difference between the peaks and troughs of a piece, the forte and pianissimo of musical composition. The contrast of morphology of the Shenzhen site creates an intriguing sequence of landscapes. The powerful rolling landscape of Lianhua Hill provides the opening section of the morphological score. From the Ceremonial Park to the Symbiotic Roof Garden through the City Hall, Tree-shaded Park and Shopping Mall the landscape becomes controlled and flat, nature tamed by man. At the Symbiotic Roof Garden the landscape works in symbiosis with the man-made structure beneath. The morphological

Information Network (Eco-Media Infrastructure)

Vehicular Network (Logistic Infrastructure)

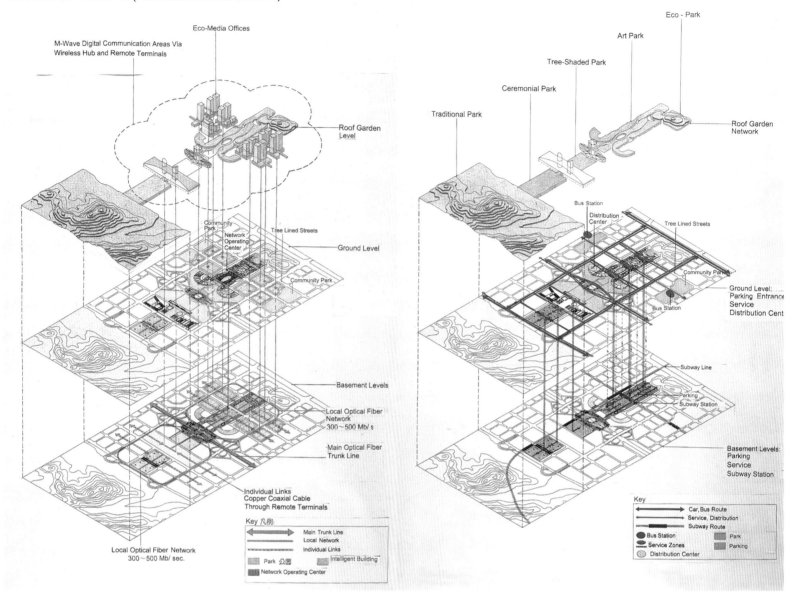

M-Wave Digital Communication Areas Via
Wireless Hub and Remote Terminals

Eco-Media Offices

Roof Garden
Level

Community
Park

Network
Operating
Center

Tree Lined Streets

Ground Level

Community Park

Basement Levels

Local Optical Fiber
Network
300~500 Mb/ s

Main Optical Fiber
Trunk Line

Individual Links
Copper Coaxial Cable
Through Remote Terminals

Local Optical Fiber Network
300~500 Mb/ sec.

Key 凡例:

Main Trunk Line
Local Network
Individual Links
Park 公園
Intelligent Building
Network Operating Center

Eco - Park
Art Park
Tree-Shaded Park
Ceremonial Park
Traditional Park

Roof Garden
Network

Bus Station
Distribution
Center

Tree Lined Streets

Community Park

Ground Level:
Parking Entrance
Service
Distribution Center

Bus Station

Subway Line

Parking
Subway Station

Basement Levels:
Parking
Service
Subway Station

Key

Car, Bus Route
Service, Distribution
Subway Route
Bus Station
Service Zones
Distribution Center
Park
Parking

Urban Score

OPPOSITE TOP: Information and vehicular networks
BELOW: Urban Score, Concept and linear diagram
OVERLEAF: Model

Urban Score: Concept

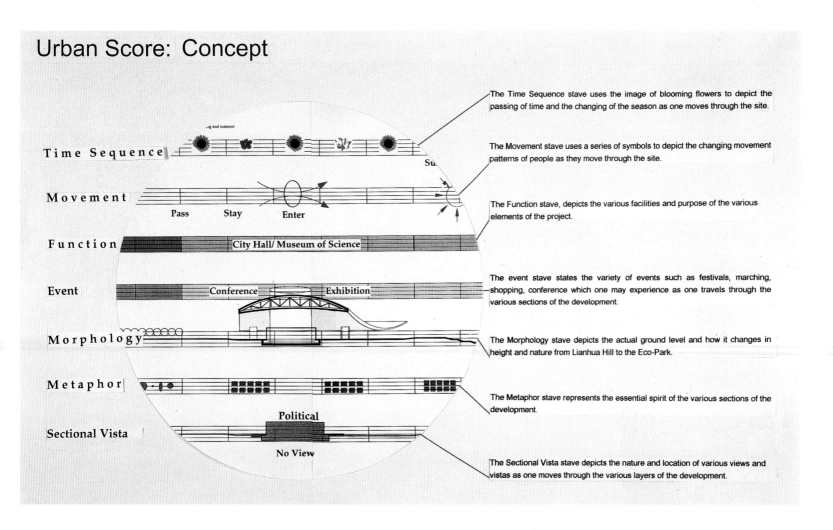

Time Sequence — The Time Sequence stave uses the image of blooming flowers to depict the passing of time and the changing of the season as one moves through the site.

Movement — The Movement stave uses a series of symbols to depict the changing movement patterns of people as they move through the site.

Pass   Stay   Enter

Function — City Hall/ Museum of Science — The Function stave, depicts the various facilities and purpose of the various elements of the project.

Event — Conference   Exhibition — The event stave states the variety of events such as festivals, marching, shopping, conference which one may experience as one travels through the various sections of the development.

Morphology — The Morphology stave depicts the actual ground level and how it changes in height and nature from Lianhua Hill to the Eco-Park.

Metaphor — The Metaphor stave represents the essential spirit of the various sections of the development.

Sectional Vista — Political — No View — The Sectional Vista stave depicts the nature and location of various views and vistas as one moves through the various layers of the development.

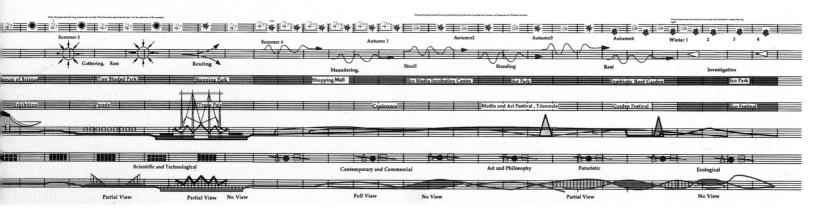

Urban Design

composition is punctuated at the end by the Eco-Park sited on a slight hill.

Movement
The movement of people will change according to the environment and enclosure of the spaces. A walk from Lianhua Hill to the Eco-Park in the Shenzhen development provides a full spectrum of movement patterns from strolling, to marching, to resting, gathering and entering, creating a rich experience. For instance, the morphology of Lianhua Hill suggests a strolling movement as people walk around the Chinese gardens and follow paths along the natural contour of the land. In the Ceremonial Park there is a marching rhythm as the landscape is punctuated by a regular tree landscape. The City Hall is a gateway to the rest of the site and here the movement is entering. The Tree-shaded Park is a place of gathering and rest.

Function
Shenzhen development offers a number of essential facilities to ensure a complete, efficient and advanced urban environment. The Chinese Garden provides a traditional start to the composition. The Ceremonial Park is a park for cultural and ceremonial events and festivals. The City Hall provides an essential administrative centre for the city, adjacent to a Science Museum. The Shopping Park provides the venue for a conglomeration of shops specializing in high-tech software and audio-visual and media equipment. The Media Incubation Centre contains a Research Centre, Education Centre, New Business Starter Centre, and Media Software Development Centre. The Art/Media/ Shopping Mall comprises an Art Museum, Media Park, and Shopping Mall. The Symbiotic Garden provides flowing natural green space along the axis of the development. The Tree-Shaded Park is to be used for gathering and informal events.

Events
There are many venues for a vibrant array of events and festivals. For example, Lianhua Hill is the locus of a Traditional Festival; the Ceremonial Park will hold parades; and the City Hall and Science Museum, conferences and exhibitions.

Metaphor
Along the north-south axis, the parks embody wider cultural and societal themes. Each park area is a metaphor on various themes: Natural, Cultural, Political, Scientific and Technological, Commercial, Artistic and Philosophical, Futuristic and Biological.

Vista
The space is also planned through vistas. At 90° to the North-South Park Axis, views out to the surrounding city have been planned so that vistas come in and out of view: full view, partial view, no view. Along the North-South

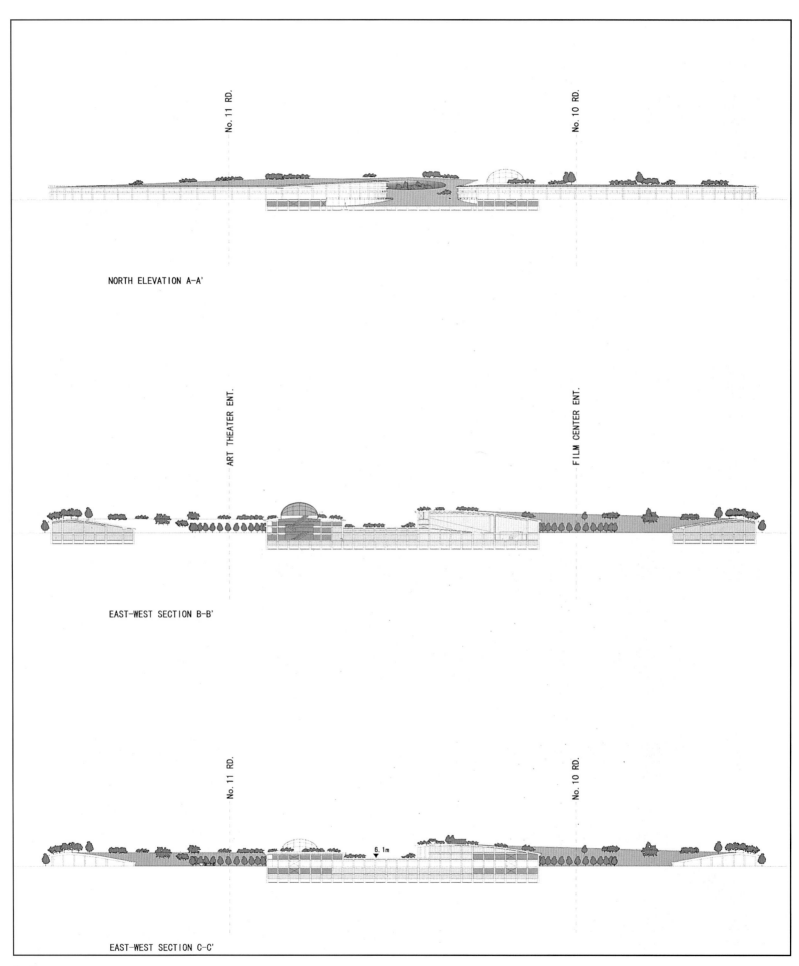

NORTH ELEVATION A-A'

EAST-WEST SECTION B-B'

EAST-WEST SECTION C-C'

Sections

Axis various special vistas and viewpoints have been provided: a view of the Ceremonial Park towards Lianhua Hill; a view of the Incubation Centre from Crystal Island; a view of the Art Centre.

Within the shopping mall of the PSSCA, pocket parks have been provided at strategic locations to provide areas for rest and and to permit views out to the city as well as light into the basement shopping areas.

SCALE COMPARISON

The Shenzhen design provides an urban environment comparable in scale and variety to the great urban centres across the globe, such as the Champs Elysées in Paris. Shenzhen multi-complex is on a scale equivalent to, if not larger than, the Louvre. However the scheme has been broken into a variety of sections on a human scale in accordance with the urban score.

Walking through the Shenzhen site from Lianhua Hill to the Eco-Park provides the pedestrian with a series of walks through a variety of spaces, connected by nodes and focal points, such as the Art Park, the Shopping Park, the City Hall, the Ceremonial Park.

ECO-PARK/WATER LANDSCAPE

Eco-Park

Terminating the North-South Axis of the site is a special park exhibiting the symbiosis of man and nature. This Eco-Park will feature dense forest habitat: rivers, rock features, areas for eco-recreation and educational eco-tours, and net enclosures for small animals and birds. The Eco-Park will generate its own revenue by charging entrance fees similar to botanical gardens.

Eco Recreation
Unobtrusive Net Enclosure: Okinawa, Nago Nature Park
Small Animal Habitat: Nagasaki Bio Park
Computer-guided Educational Eco-Tour
Bird Enclosure
Natural Drainage
Water Landscape

The PSSCA will use water as a design feature at strategic points. The Traditional Park, Eco-Park, and central Crystal Island prominently use water landscaping.

Traditional Park
Crystal Island Waterfall
Eco-Park Water Features

GREEN NETWORK
Roof Garden Network
Traditional Park
Ceremonial Park
Tree-shaded Park
Art Park
Eco-Park
Street Level Green Network
Community Park

Tree-lined Streets
Basement Level
Node

PEDESTRIAN NETWORK

Roof Level	Second Level
Pedestrian Bridge	Pedestrian Bridge
Roof Garden Park	Shopping Mall
Eco-Media Office	Shopping Podium
Ground Level	**Basement Levels**
Shopping Mall	Shopping Mall
Shopping Podium	Subway Station
Tree-lined Streets	Parking

VEHICULAR NETWORK
(LOGISTIC INFRASTRUCTURE)

Roof Garden Network
Traditional Park
Ceremonial Park
Tree-shaded Park
Art Park
Eco-Park
Community Park

Ground Level	Basement Levels
Parking Entrance	Service
Parking	Distribution Centre
Service	Bus Station
Subway Station	Tree-lined Streets

INFORMATION NETWORK
(ECO-MEDIA INFRASTRUCTURE)

Roof Garden Level
M-Wave Digital Communication Areas via Wireless Hub and Remote Terminals
Eco-Media Offices
Ground Level
Community Park
Tree-lined Streets
Network Operating Centre
Basement Levels
Main Optical Fibre Trunk Line 1-30 GB/sec.
Local Optical Fibre Network 300-500 MB/sec.
Individual Links Copper Coaxial Cable through Remote Terminals

ECO-TECHNOLOGY

Sky Garden
Through the use of advanced man-made soils, a lightweight and biologically effective roof-top garden will be produced.

Grass-Spacers
The combination of water permeable pavers and grass provides a durable material for use in large plazas such as the gathering space of the Tree-shaded Park. The grass-spacers ensure a cool surface even in hot weather.

Rainwater Permeable Pavement
Roads should be constructed with pavement that permits the permeation of water.

Air Cleaning Through Soil
Filtering systems which use the soil of the

parking structures and roof gardens will control CO_2 emissions from automobiles.

Rainwater Recycling System
Water recycling systems, such as rainwater storage tanks, will be used.

Garbage Compactor
The garbage from the institutions will produce fuel using the garbage compactor that will be used for the electric generating incinerator.

Solar Panels
Solar battery power may be used as an example to the new community of Eco-Technology.

LIGHTING AND FURNITURE

Lighting Plan
Various night-time lighting methods will be used to make use of the natural and architectural characteristics of each area.
By lighting up the traditional architecture in the Traditional Chinese Garden, one can perceive the entire mountain at night.
In the Art Park, lighting will be provided to emphasize the various features, and bright light will come through the gaps and entrances.

Out of consideration for the birds and animals in the Eco-Park, the surroundings of the park will be dimly lit, so that the natural landscape may be glimpsed at both the northern and southern ends of the central axis.

Stone Pavement: Approach Light
Indirect Lighting for Traditional Architecture
Lighting Colonnade
Flag Pole Dotted Mid-Height Street Lamp

Flower Bed: Approach Light
Street Lighting – more than usual by indirect lighting against the Giant Roof
Pocket Rest Space

Staircase: Approach Light
Light against Trees
Overflow of Light from Crystal Island

Pavement: Access Light
Telecom Media Access Points
Glow of Strong Garden Light
Floodlighting from the Gap
Overflow of Light from the Entrances
Street Lighting – stronger than usual

Eco-Park: Surrounded by Dim Light.

REFERENCE: PARK SCALE COMPARISONS
Central Park, New York
Shenzhen PSSCA
Washington Mall, Washington D.C.
Ueno Park, Tokyo

ABOVE: K Museum, view from the west
RIGHT: Fibre Wave at K Museum

Makoto-Sei Watanabe

The Fibre Wave, K Museum

The topography – contrast and interchange

The complex topographical form of the K Museum comes from a combination of its undulating base structure and the building itself. But whereas the building is made of rectangular units and in such a way as to reflect light, the base structure is composed of three-dimensional waving surfaces, and covered with a light-absorbing black material. The sharp contrast between these two elements is fundamental to the museum.

One of the features of such contrasting extremes is that each pole acknowledges that part of itself which can be found in the other. This is known as "interchangeability." In this work, the light upper part of the building appears as "chips" of reflected metal visible among the black waves, and part of this dark wave becomes a semi-transparent, curved volume partially buried in the metal wall of the lighter building above.

The black area under the building is quite solid, covered with stone and tile, housing a water supply plant and supporting the

shining building above. Yet its undulating shape makes the building look as if it were drifting among black waves. The waves are pierced with slender silver lines that seem to whirl in the wind. Together they make up an environment of sculptures, called "Touching the Wind," which acts as an interface between the solid, motionless building and the undulating topography.

"The Fibre Wave" – Designless Design

I wanted to create something lithe for the museum's landscape, something like trees swaying and rustling, or grasslands rippling like waves in the wind. Living things, even plants firmly rooted in the soil, are never completely motionless. Their position and form constantly change in response to wind, rain, temperature, and light. They position themselves in such a way as to lose the least amount of energy under any given set of conditions. We humans almost derive a sense of pleasure when we see them wasting nothing in their unpretentious and earnest

will to live. The beauty of living things comes from these mechanisms for survival.

My purpose with this project was to create a landscape that possesses such primal beauty. Nevertheless, approximating the mechanisms of living organisms by artificial means requires using the most advanced human technology such as carbon fibre, solar cells, and bright, light-emitting diodes. I created the "fibre wave." A forest of long carbon fibre rods dances in the wind like grass in a field, while the blue lights at the tips of the solar-cell-powered light-emitting diodes sway back and forth like fireflies. Naturally, these movements are not something that can be tightly controlled by the designer. They are directed only by their arrangement and the wind. The "shape" of such movement cannot be – and is not – designed; it is continuously generated in response to the forces and laws of nature, and the nature of the materials involved. Such landscape is, then, the result of a "designless design."

M-SW

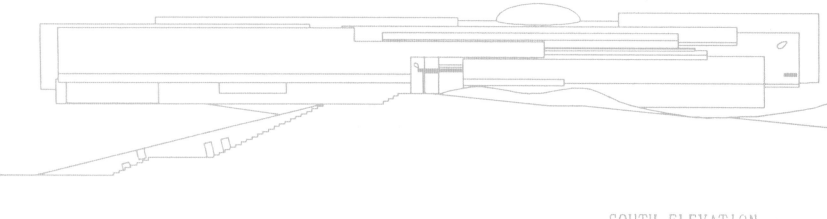

SOUTH ELEVATION

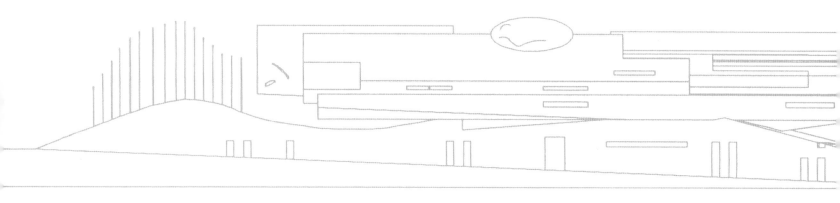

NORTH ELVATION

BELOW: The Fibre Wave in Motion

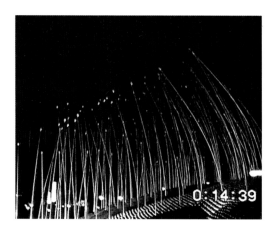

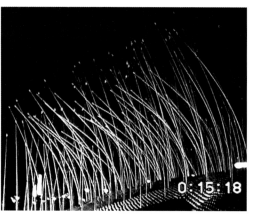

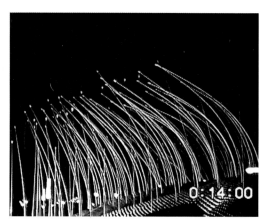

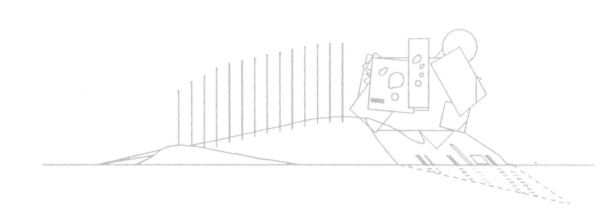

EAST ELEVATION

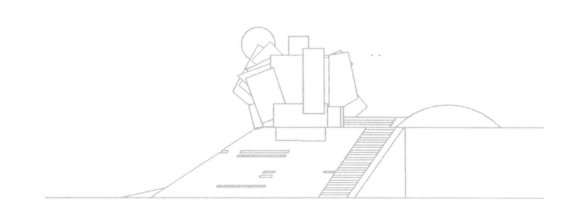

WEST ELEVATION

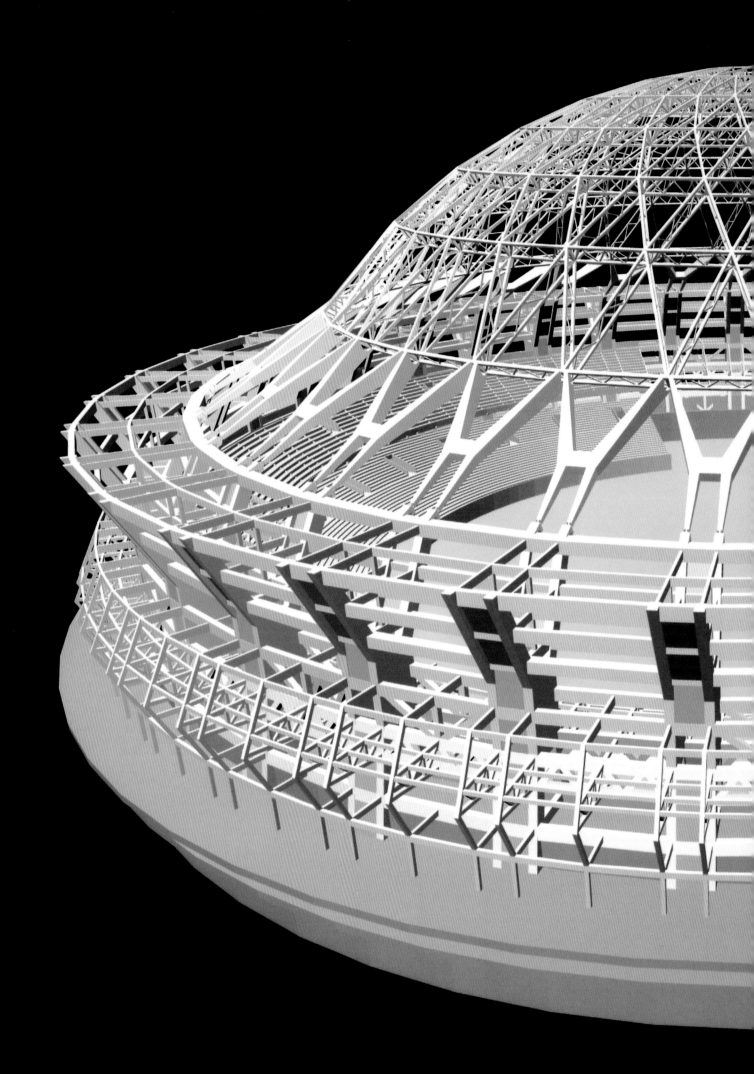

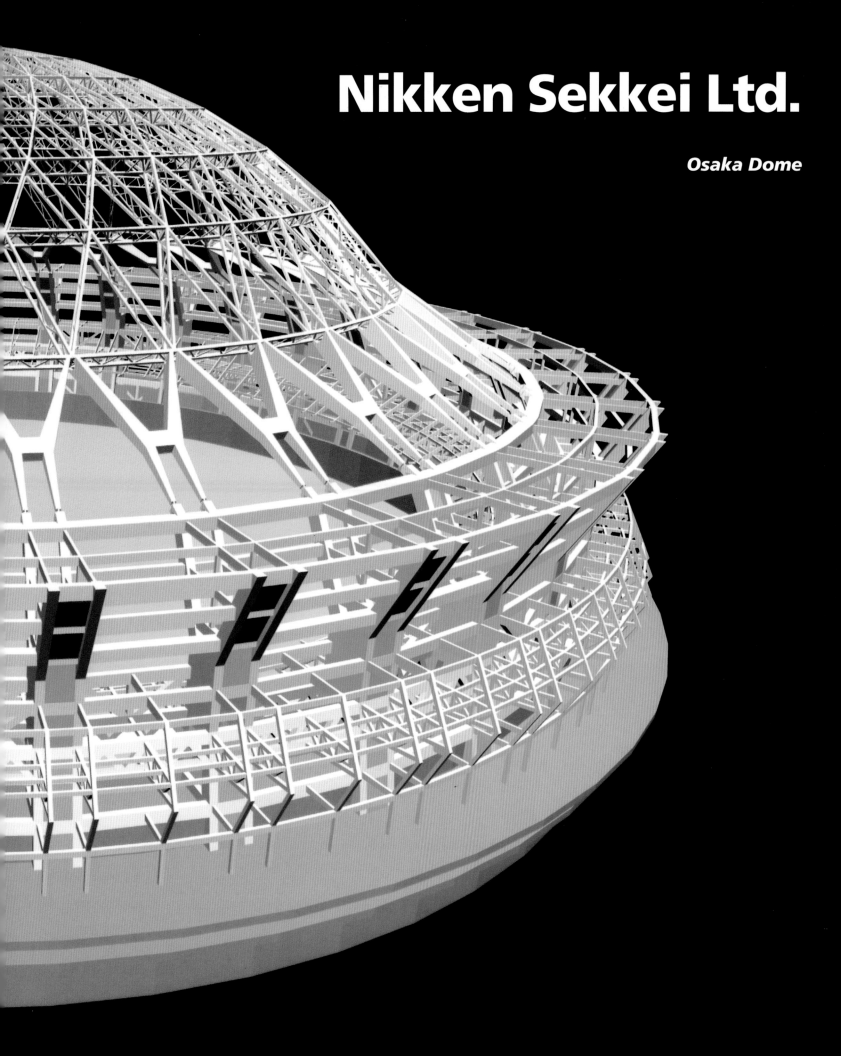

PAGES 108-109: Configuration when the super rings are lowered for baseball in a shaded environment. PAGES 110-111: A new landmark for Osaka; ABOVE AND RIGHT: Indoor view of sporting events.

Design Outline

The Osaka Dome is a multi-purpose dome with a seating capacity of 44,000 for sports events, and a maximum seating capacity of 55,000 for other events. Visually, the dome's exterior is dominated by the Fiesta Mall, forming a floating skyline of waves and clouds, but which also has a practical function as a venue for events apart from those of the dome itself. Inside, the dome has a mechanized system that can change the arena and seating space configurations to suit the event taking place. The ceiling shape is also extremely flexible; it is composed of layers of ring-shaped elements (called "super-rings") which can be raised and lowered as necessary to create whatever acoustic effect is desired.

Structural Design

The Dome's roof consists of a 134m diameter centre dome portion and a 16m wide perimeter in the shape of the brim of a hat. The perimeter has a more gentle slope than the central dome. Structurally, the roof framing consists of the central dome, which is designed to form a uniform geometry of steel lamella, and a perimeter portion composed of thirty-six pairs of Y-shaped steel girders laid out uniformly. The cases of these girders are located on top of the stands.

The dome's deadweight, which is about 7,000 tons, creates numerous stresses. Compressive stresses are caused in both the radial and perimeter directions of the centre dome portion while compressive and bending stresses are developed in the perimeter. Intensive stresses which develop at the borderline area between the centre and the perimeter are taken care of by the compression ring beam.

Other stresses caused by the deadweight are carried to the substructure by way of the hinged dome bases. Since these hinged bases are interconnected by the tension ring beam and great lateral force is carried by tension hoops, almost no lateral force is transferred to the stand structure below.

The stand structure under the domed roof is of steel framed reinforced concrete construction. From the viewpoint of architectural planning as well as exterior aesthetics, the structure in the radical direction consists of Y-shaped frames which have comparatively low rigidity. On the other hand, the frame in the circumferential direction has shear walls to ensure high rigidity and strength. The frame in the radial direction and that in the circumferential direction are integrated into one by the floor slab that extends in the circumferential direction to form a strong, rigid structure which looks like a large doughnut.

Outline of the Construction

The steel members of the dome were erected by the lift-up method. They were lifted into place by wires manipulated from thirty-six erection platforms. Stresses and deformation of the members at principal locations were measured while these lifting operations were performed.

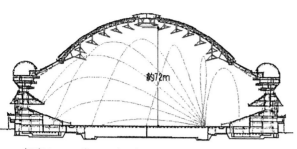

採光1　スポーツ（野球・アメリカンフットボール）

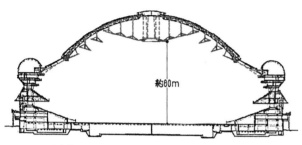

遮光1　コンサート（5、3.5万人）・野球

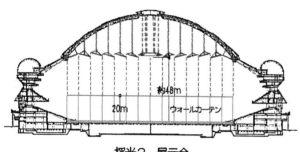

採光2　展示会

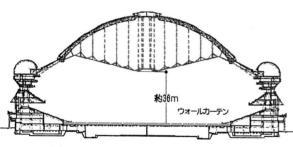

遮光1　コンサート（3.5・2万人）式典

RIGHT: Polycarbonate roof for natural lighting, approx.
76m in diameter. FROM TOP TO BOTTOM: Lighting 1 (for
sports: baseball and American football); Shading 1 (for
concerts – 35,000 to 50,000 people – and baseball);
Lighting 2 (for exhibitions); Shading 2 (for concerts –
20,000 to 35,000 people – and ceremonies)

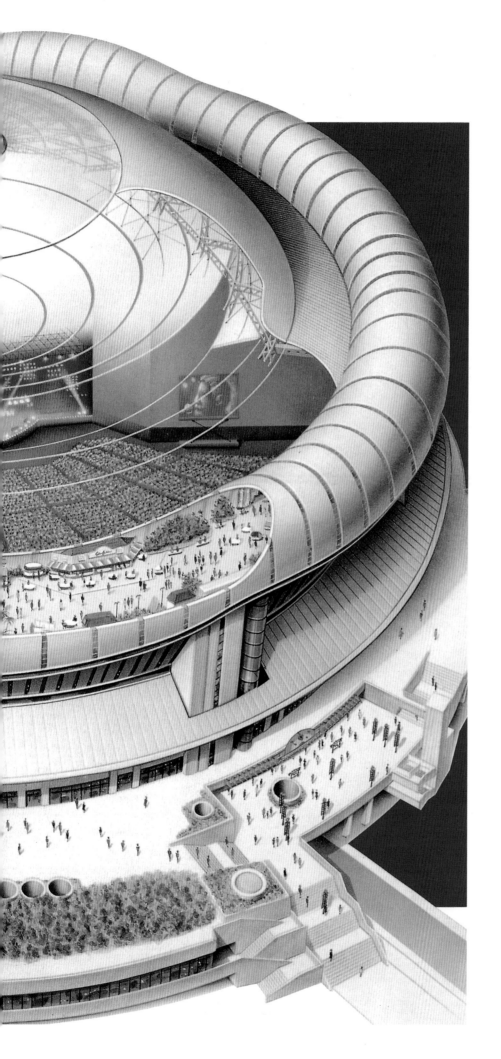

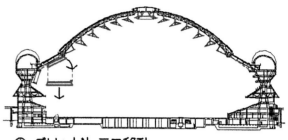

① グリッドトラス移動

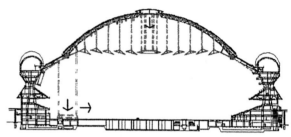

② グリッドトラス降下・移動
スーパーリング降下

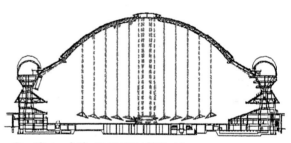

③ グリッドトラス吊り物取付
ウォールカーテン取付

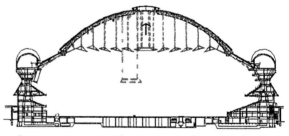

④ スーパーリング・ウォールカーテン上昇
グリッドトラス上昇

FROM TOP TO BOTTOM: Grid-truss movement; Grid-truss descent and movement (super ring lowered); Grid-truss suspension and wall curtains installed; Wall curtains installed on super rings (grid-truss raised)

RIGHT TOP: Exterior close-up. RIGHT BOTTOM: Interior view, entertainment street. BELOW: All the artificial turf, including the periphery, can be completely coiled within 90 minutes, significantly reducing the time required to create a new setting. Sequence (from left to right): coiling flow chart; the artificial turf is first coiled from the edges; the coiling pit cover opens to begin coiling; during coiling; coiling almost complete; coiling complete. OPPOSITE: Aerial view. OVERLEAF: Indoor view of a concert attended by 20,000 people

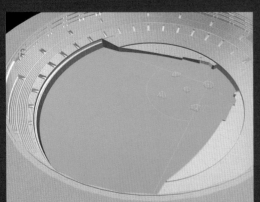
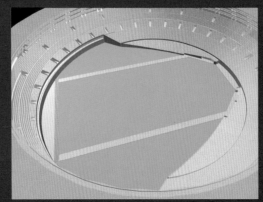
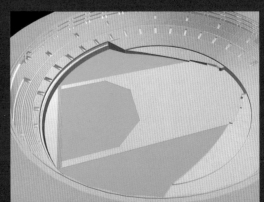

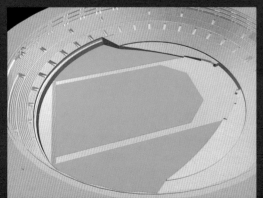
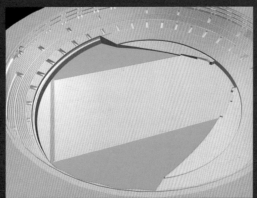
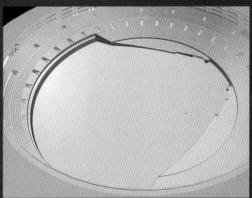

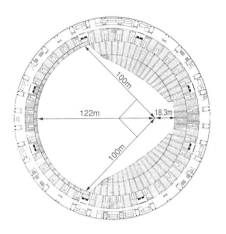 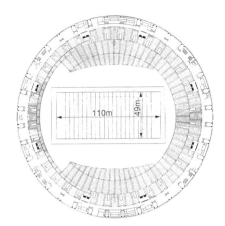 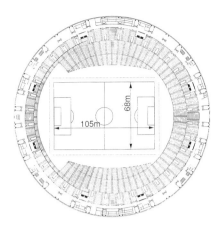

ABOVE: Movable seats permit the arena shape to be changed according to the event (from left to right: baseball, American football, soccer). RIGHT: Night view of the stadium. BOTTOM: Detailed section. OPPOSITE PAGE, TOP LEFT: Elevation. RIGHT: Flexible partitioned arena, arrangements (from top to bottom) for 20,000, for 35,000 and for 50,000 people. MIDDLE: The Super Rings fully lowered for concerts and other events requiring a more subdued atmosphere BOTTOM LEFT: The configuration when the Super Rings are lowered so baseball can be played in a shaded environment. BOTTOM RIGHT: The configuration when the Super Rings are raised to allow maximum natural lighting during a baseball game

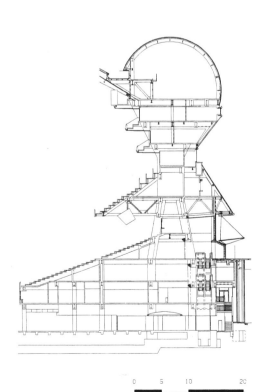

0   5   10   20

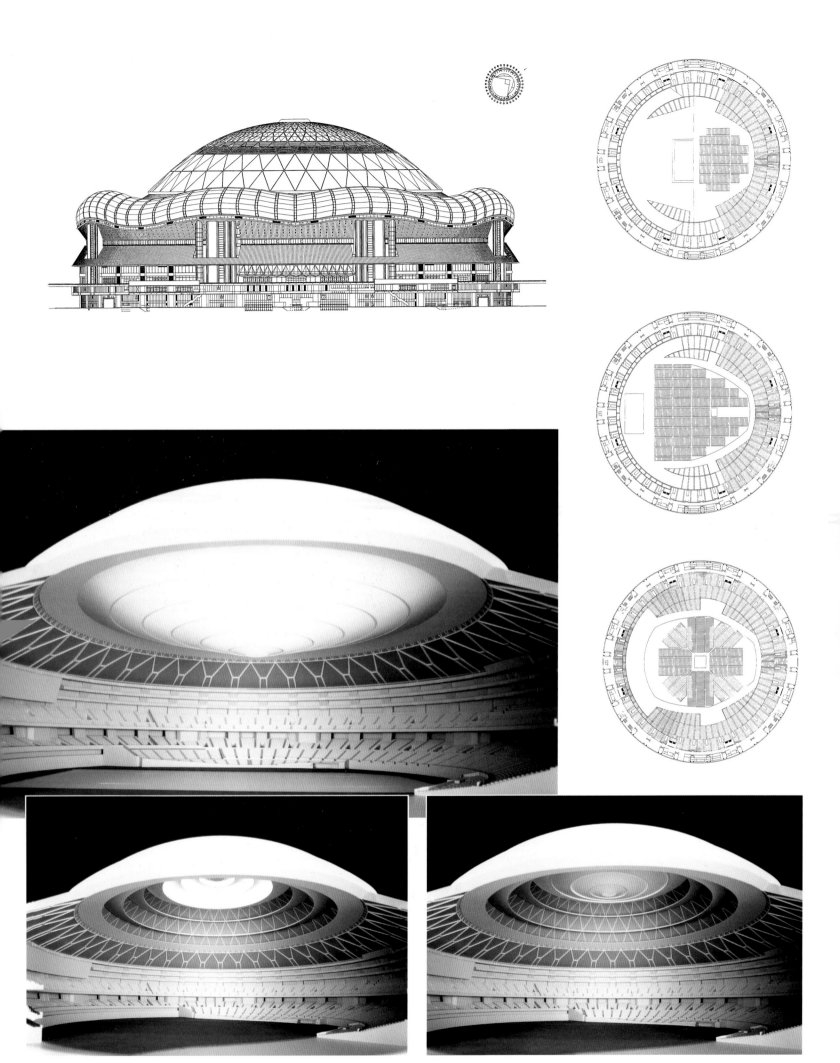

The Schools

Tokyo Institute of Technology (TIT)

The Department of Architecture and Building Engineering at TIT – established in 1902 with the first students arriving in 1907 – offers a varied curriculum which connects diverse areas of architectural studies: Architectural Design, Architectural History, Architectural Planning, Structural Engineering, Soil Engineering, Environmental Engineering, Material Engineering, etc. Lectures and classes are given by respected specialists in these various faculties of architectural studies.

For the bachelor's degree course, made up of around seventy students a year, the architectural curriculum starts in the second year and ends in the fourth for the bachelor's degree. To start with students gain a basic knowledge of architecture and fundamental skills of design. In the third year, they spend much more time learning about construction, and how to present their own ideas through architectural design. In the fourth year, most time is devoted to the thesis and diploma project. Students become members of a specific laboratory which covers the subject of their thesis, headed by an advising professor. The thesis is developed under the direction of this professor, but the diploma project is developed by the student himself or herself, and most are presented in the Architectural Institute of Japan.

Over 60% of students continue their studies in the same laboratory during the two year Master's course. Architectural design is offered by few special laboratories during the Master's programme, although by now more than half of the students choose to focus on other other topics. For instance, more students get involved in scientific research and high level engineering, on which TIT places particular emphasis.

TIT has a remarkable system for teaching architectural design. First of all, the Department of Architecture and Building Engineering boasts a tradition of employing "Architect-Professors." Yoshiro Taniguchi, Kiyoshi Seike, Kazuo Shinohara, and Kazumasa Yamashita, very important architects in the course of modern Japanese architecture, have all taught at TIT, while conducting their own design practices in their university studios. Instead of having a private office outside the school, these professors worked with their students on actual projects, just like a scientific research laboratory. Students, in addition to studying in classes, can learn about design and the profession by working with their architect-professors on real projects. The tradition is still strong today, with several distinguished professors, such as Mitsuru Senda, Kazunari Sakamoto, or Koji Yagi, and younger ones, like Shinichi Okuyama and Yoshihaha Tsukamoto, teaching in this way. Through this unique tradition, theoretical studies in architecture are tied to actual projects. This system continues to produce remarkable studies on architectural space, architectural discourse, and urban issues.

Secondly, the third-year design course is a series of intensive studio projects led by several active Japanese architects. Last year, Kazuyo Sejima, Kengo Kuma, Takefumi Aida, Koji Takeda, taught design and discussed related issues with students. Themes given by these architects are innovative to foster critical approaches to design. Some, such as "Architecture with $100,000" (Sejima), and "How to spend 5,000,000,000 Yen in Okinawa" (Kuma) have provoked hypothetical studies in context and architectural scale, measured, uncustomarily, by volume or budget. Others, such as "Schools as public facilities" (Aida), and "Urban housing with function-X" (Takeda) have criticised conventional forms in these general building types, and proposed new formations to suit today's social and urban context. These design courses strongly focus on the interaction between context and architectural structure, on the interrelationship between different spatial definitions, and on the interdependence between the building and a highly complex built environment, such as Tokyo.

Thirdly, the results of these design courses are presented in the design journal "ka," published in each semester by the TIT Society of Architectural Design Education (a kind of alumni association of architects from TIT). This journal, edited by a committee of teachers with contributions from students, reports on the jury of every design studio, including each student's projects and their criticism by teachers, visiting lecturers and other students. Each issue also has special articles on news and events and current projects.

Yoshiharu Taukamoto

A Process of Re-Weaving by Tappei Ito

This proposal is located in south-east Shinjuku and is surrounded by various elements of Tokyo's urban fabric, such as Meiji Street, the Yamanote train line and Shinjuku Park. The buildings which currently stand on this site do not particularly interact with these lines of movement. So this project is set up as an experiment with form to discover new possibilities within the specific nature of urban flow.

The final project utilizes both views and connections studied in previous system models, together with the selected enveloping forms, which allows the observer to engage with the environment in a multilevel, interactive way.

Office for Short Stay
by Hidetaka Yoshimura

The project is situated at a point of multiple boundaries. To the west is a residential area, to the east is an industrial area and a horse racing track. The building links the canal to the north with the park on reclaimed land to the south. The proposed temporary office, with supporting facilities, aims to work with the fluid, changing nature of this site.

The office building is composed of various units such as an office to rent, lecture rooms, libraries and the public spaces of a pier and a pedestrian bridge. Each unit has a narrow width on the ground level (approximately 3.5m) to allow equal and direct entry from the street. However, the upper levels of each unit respond individually to various requirements, creating cohesive elements within a complicated whole.

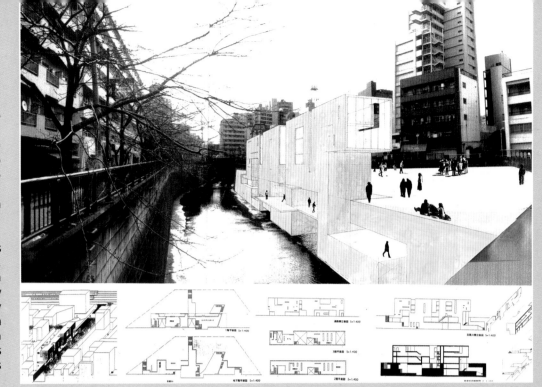

Service Area at East-Ginza
by Koichi Endo

Ginza-Ramp is a neighbourhood straddling the crossing of Metropolitan Expressway C-1 and Harumi Street. The expressway is submerged at the level of an old canal, while Harumi Street links Ginza and neighbouring areas at ground level. The wider area is one of the most animated in Tokyo. But "Ginza-Ramp" is divided into two parts, so few pedestrians are seen there even in daytime. My proposal was to cover this expressway with a 350m long building acting as a service area. Usually such a building serves the expressway, but here it includes both a motor pool and various cultural and commercial facilities, acting as a connector for the divided area. The motor pool is a tube supported over the expressway by a series of iron truss beams. Small shops are lodged between the beams at street level, and various cultural and commercial facilities are arranged on top of the tube.

Study for Meguro river
by Daiju Nagaoka

A library, a gallery, a rental building, a studio and a theatre; these five independent buildings are set into a rhythm of existing bridges across a small urban river. These buildings can work independently, as a complex, or as part of the urban flow.

For example, the rows of cherry trees along the river work at the scale of the city, but can also be seen as a lobby for the whole complex. Existing shops, cafes, car parks and so on lead smoothly into sections of the project, making the definition of the edge to each building ambiguous, and giving a sense of distance between each part of the complex. Through this series of studies, this project raises questions about the interdependence of architecture and the specifics of the built environment.

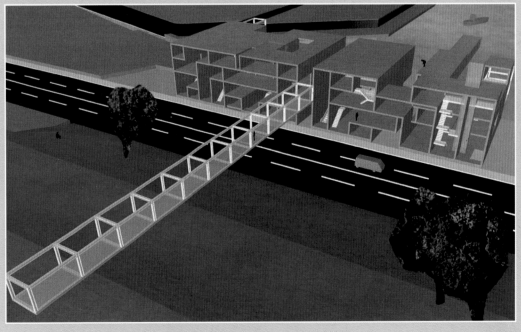

~ 2 ~
A stairway to Torii

~ 1 ~
Entry

~ 3 ~
The beginning of Torii

~ 5 ~
The end of Torii

~ 4 ~
Middle of Torii

~ 6 ~
Wood square lumbers
Many directions appear.

Jin Shimoda (graduate course)

Project: ZEN Bridge Project in Vico Morte
(Exchange Program with SCI-ARC '97)

Instructor: Takefumi Aida/Betta Terragni/ Michael Dolinski

What is Zen? Realization of self.
How does on realize oneself? By the
movement of one's body.

Program

1. Torii
To attain a sense of exaltation, wending one's
way through successive shrine gates.

2. Squared wood trunks
To discern the truth of one's identity,
traversing a forest of squared wood trunks,
erected along oblique transcending lines.
Here paths branch out in various directions.
We become lost, so move erratically.

3. Meditation room
In a darkened room, light filters in through
narrow gaps, and amid the sound of a
stream, we engage in profound
contemplation. Here, static in this room, we
gain a recognition of self.

Jun Nagane (Graduate course)

Project: Urban Interstice (a "Sports Club for Somnambulists")

Instructor: Hiromi Fujii

Tokyo, a city highly symbolic of today's society,
is regarded as important only as a place for
high density living and consumption. Human
beings living in the city are increasingly
regarded as statistics representing density,
endlessly sleepwalking from "point" to
"point." This project proposes a device to
establish a new connection between human
beings and the city. Space was planned based
on the relationship between human beings
and the "line" connecting "point" to "point."

The design programme is as follows.
1. Solid: the density of the contemporary city
will be traced.
2. Void: this will be transformed into
nothingness.
3. Surface: a place that is neither solid nor void
will be created.

As a result of this performance, new events will
occur and a new means of communication will
begin operating in the contemporary city.

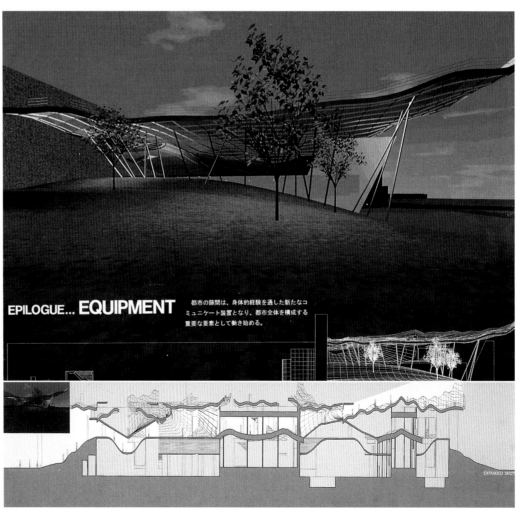

EPILOGUE... **EQUIPMENT**　都市の隙間は、身体的経験を通した新たなコ
ミュニケート装置となり、都市全体を構成する
重要な要素として働き始める。

Rintaro Yabe (Graduate course)

Project: Rewinded Passage

Instructor: Hiromi Fujii / Masanori Kei

Today, as the digital network becomes an increasingly important social environment, each networker is an "Alice-in-Wonderland-figure" transcending place and time to visit and explore diverse worlds. In encounters with the network, we need to have a will and a consciousness of our own.

A space like a Klein bottle will be constructed. Paths criss-crossing in spirals will be created inside the architecture. As a consequence, people will become involved in many happenings. A passage that includes the city and the nearby environment will be formed because the interior and the exterior will become continuous.

The educational policy of the school, put simply, aims to develop a wide range of capable people who can adapt to the present state of architecture. Instruction is offered in a number of separate, specialist fields including design, structure, production, environment and mechanical systems, in line with architectural education throughout Japan.

Design education is generally intended to synthesize these fields, although we probably give it even greater emphasis than at other institutions. Broadly speaking, it is divided into undergraduate and graduate courses, four years long and two years long, respectively. In the undergraduate course, the focus is on letting students acquire design skills, and on teaching them how those skills are closely related to society, the economy, engineering and culture. Themes and methods differ from studio to studio. In my own studio, we examine the significance of architecture for human beings, a basic theme of architecture, based on the study and analysis of modern architecture in Europe and Japanese architectural history. Diverse architectural issues are studied, at present, from the perspective of the human body. Outside experts and architects are invited, and lectures, symposiums and workshops are held to deal more broadly with those issues.

There are approximately ten design studios belonging to two faculties in this school. Usually students enter the studios of their choice in their fourth undergraduate year, and also if they go on to graduate school for two years. The design studios are all very individualistic and have different themes of research. Yet one of the unifying charactersists of graduate education is the communication of ideas with overseas schools. At present, there are exchange programmes with the Southern California Institute of Architecture (SCI-Arc), the Moscow Architectural Institute (MARKHI) and the School of Architecture of Paris-Belleville (EAPB). This year about ten graduate students will stay for one month at the Moscow Architectural Institute and together with local students design an urban complex for a historic district in the Russian capital. In April, thirteen students from the School of Architecture of Paris-Belleville stayed at Shibauru for a month and a half to design, with seven of our students, a housing project for about fifty households in a so-called "low-city" district of Tokyo.

We call this exchange programme and workshop the "Paris-Tokyo-Moscow travelling studio." It offers an opportunity to gain a deeper understanding of different culture and society, vital in an age when architectural and city-planning work is becoming increasingly international in character. It is hoped that the programme will foster a more fundamental and global approach in the consideration of architectural, urban and environmental spaces.

Hiromi Fujii

University of Tokyo

Many outstanding Japanese architects have graduated from the University of Tokyo (Todai), the oldest university in Japan, including such internationally renowned contemporary designers as Kenzo Tange, Fumihiko Maki, Hiroshi Hara, and Toyo Ito. In turn, several prominent architects have taught here, including Japan's three Pritzker Prize-winning architects, Tange, Maki, and Tadao Ando.

Todai has relatively few architecture students (60 undergraduate and graduate students in each year of study, of which about 50 per cent – or 30 graduate students per year) – major in design). The undergraduate course lasts four years. In the first one-and-a-half years, students are required to study at the Faculty of Liberal Arts; therefore, they have only two-and-a-half years to study architecture professionally. This starts in the winter semester of their second year, with students taking an introductory course in design. Then, they are required to submit six projects between the summer semesters of their third and fourth years. Students have six weeks to complete each one of these projects. In the final winter semester, students are expected to submit both a graduation design thesis and a graduation research thesis. Our postgraduate program, while designed mostly to educate researchers and university teachers, has a similar structure, with students expected to write a thesis even if they major in design.

The department has exceptional educational facilities. We have separate studio and study rooms for both undergraduate and graduate students, special rooms for juries, an exhibition space, a lecture hall, and a department library with a large collection of architectural books and periodicals. There are thirty-five permanent and about twelve visiting professors, which include, alongside several "star" professors, practitioners, painters, and others who are all outstanding in their own fields.

However, this does not necessarily mean that Todai has a special or excellent education system for architects. Indeed, from an international perspective, it is difficult to claim that we at Todai have an adequate architectural education. This is perhaps more the fault of the Japanese tradition of architectural education. In common with most other universities in Japan, Todai's department of architecture is part of the Faculty of Engineering. As a result, the curriculum's major fields of study are engineering subjects like Structural Analysis, Building Construction, Mechanical Engineering, Environmental Science, Material Engineering and so on, in addition to (and often above) Architectural Design, Architectural Planning, and the History of Architecture. Not surprisingly, most of our graduates in architecture find jobs in the construction-related industries. So, for at least half of them, the graduation thesis project is probably the final opportunity to design architecture rather than pure engineering. It might be said that, in regard to the knowledge of architecture and building, Japanese departments of architecture impart to their graduates a rather general skill of integrating and solving complex problems in modern society. Needless to say, it is our long term aim at Todai to diversify this currently inadequate architectural education to reflect the breadth of interests upon which architecture touches.

Another significant characteristic of Japanese architectural education is the dominance of building and planning science. This field of study aims at developing new planning methods for the built-environment; it is characterized by its strong interest in socio-scientific approaches and social policies, which have an undeniable influence on the architectural education in Japan. As a matter of fact, design studios in this field in many departments of architecture in Japan, are taught by scholars of whom few, if anyone at all, is actually a practising architect or by professors who have no background in practice at all. This field evidently has a considerable influence even on the practising architect-professors, since they evaluate student projects neither with the realistic approaches of actual economics or commercial feasibility, nor with the ones that are based on strong aesthetics. On the other hand, those projects that have been conceived primarily with ideas about society or attitudes of social idealism, are evaluated most highly. The question of architectural style is accepted as a matter of personal taste, while addressing more important issues is considered only appropriate in architectural publications. It is disappointing that they are not discussed with the students or in juries. Our professors are very generous in giving advice and encouraging students to develop their own ideas, but are overly careful about not to providing or imposing any of their own thinking on the students.

Moreover, architectural education in Japan displays another weakness, namely the general absence of city-planning and urban design in its curricula. Actually, Todai established a department in these related fields in the 1960s. But this Department of Urban Engineering was started by professors who, like Kenzo Tange, came from the Department of Architecture and Civil Engineering. The Department, in the wake of rapid urban expansion and deteriorating conditions in Japanese cities, responded mainly to social and engineering problems, and, while heightening the awareness of urbanism within the University as a whole, it also masked the growing absence of a serious city-planning and urban design programme in the Architecture Department; students lost the opportunity of being exposed to and learning about these fields.

More recently this department, run by professors, such as Yoshinobu Ashihara, Fumihiko Maki, Hiroshi Hara, and myself, with a more substantial interest in urban design, has had a considerable impact on our architecture programme and has compensated greatly for earlier weaknesses such that a commitment to urban design has by now become one of the strong features of Todai architecture.

On The Three Students Projects

Mr. Hironori Matubara and Ms. Emiko Tsuno were both students in the Masters course of 1997. They participated in the design studio organized by Professors Hiroshi Hara, Nagasawa, Magaribuchi, and myself. The task was to design a housing complex for 1000 habitants per hectare in the centre of Tokyo. The site was left for each student to decide.

"Housing of 4665m in Total Length" by Mr. Matubara and "Void System" by Miss Tsuno share the same basic idea, insofar as both designs rely on the use of initially simple linear masses that accommodate living spaces. These masses are then bent in various ways to generate diverse types of formal relationships and voids. Matubara uses square volumes, 4665 metres long, whereas Tsuno employs bars in a more flexible way. By bending operations Tsuno intends to connect the voids into a complex system. The resulting interplay between masses and voids weaken the boundaries between inside and outside, rendering them ambiguous. Matubara on the other hand articulates his design simply and clearly by dividing the housing complex into four stages.

The third project, titled "At the Boundary" is the graduation design of an undergraduate student, Mr.Shin Ohtake, who has received this year's Tatsuno Memorial Prize from our department. It is interesting to note that undergraduate projects are generally more feasible than graduate projects in our masters program. Ohtake's design reveals as much sophistication in manipulating surfaces, as skill in articulating or, controlling the issues of the entire site including landscaping and the relationship between the proposed building and the surrounding town.

by Dr. Hidetoshi Ohno,
Architect, Associate Professor

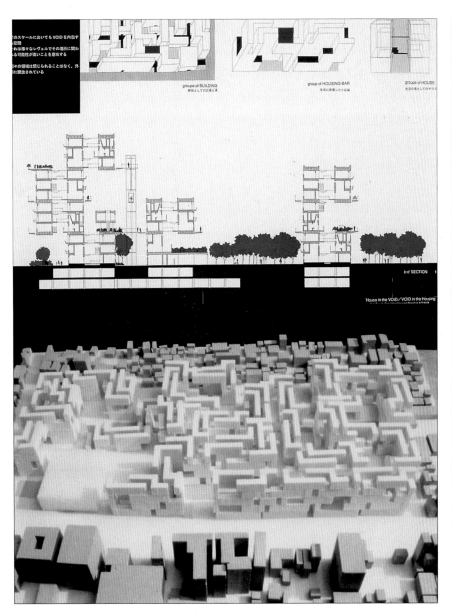

ABOVE: Hironori Matubara: "Housing of 4665m Total Length"
RIGHT: Emiko Tsuno: "Void System"
BELOW: Makoto Otake: "At the Boundary"

Ever since British engineers helped the Japanese build their first rail road line between Shimbashi in Tokyo and Yokohama in 1872, railways have played the most significant role in Japan's industrialization as well as urbanization.[1] Railroad companies in Japan typically also have real estate branches, which develop not only railway stations into important urban centres, complete with large department stores, cultural facilities, hotels, and more, but also the surrounding areas. Today Japan boasts one of the world's most developed networks of railways, which is as extensive as it is technologically advanced. It provides an exceptionally reliable service. As early as the Tokyo Olympic games in 1964, the Japanese introduced the world's first high-speed or super express train, the so-called Shinkansen line between Tokyo and Okayama, which, along the Pacific seaboard has been instrumental in the evolution of the world's largest megalopolitan development. This Tokaido Megalopolis now extends from Tokyo through Yokohama, Shizuoka, Nagoya, Kyoto, to Osaka, and even beyond, practically all the way to Fukuoka on Kyushu Island.

Throughout the years Shinkansen lines have been extended to many parts of the country, while their technological progress enabled the increase of both speed and comfort of travel. It is also remarkable how many trains provide service on these lines; on the Tokaido / Sanyo line alone there are some 210 trains running in each direction, of which 124 leave Tokyo Station daily.[2] The total number of trains leaving Tokyo on all Shinkansen lines every day reached 269 as of 1998. Nevertheless, in addition to relying on more "conventional" train technologies, Japan began to experiment with the new, magnetic levitation technology, the Maglev or linear motor train. Today only Japan and Germany continue the development of such technology. In December 1997, Japan's MLX01 train reached on its experimental Yamanashi tracks a maximum speed of 550 km per hour for an unmanned run, and a top speed of 531 km per hour for a manned run, the fastest in the world to date. With new trains introduced almost annually, Shinkansen lines, including the still experimental Maglev, are admired not only for their advanced technology and efficient service, but also for their designs, which have evolved in close relation with functionality, comfort, and the technology involved, while effectively representing the future in transportation.[3]

B. Bognar

Notes

1. It is interesting to note that British engineers, following their system back home, built the first rail lines in Japan with left hand traffic flows, and that this system was later adopted for all other modes of transportation in the country.

2. Not all trains run from Tokyo or Fukuoka, the other terminal of the 1180 km long combined Tokaido and Sanyo Shinkansen lines; many trains depart from in-between stations such Nagoya, Osaka, Okayama, etc.

3. Running tests of the Maglev train – to confirm operational stability, long-term durability, control, safety, and practicality – will continue until the end of the year 2000, when the final conclusion as to the feasibility of the new system will be reached.

Air flow around rear car.

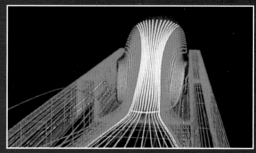

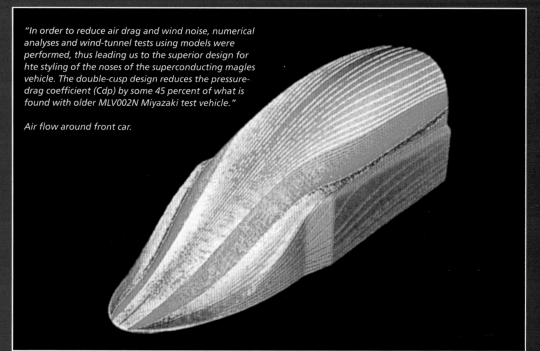

"In order to reduce air drag and wind noise, numerical analyses and wind-tunnel tests using models were performed, thus leading us to the superior design for hte styling of the noses of the superconducting magles vehicle. The double-cusp design reduces the pressure-drag coefficient (Cdp) by some 45 percent of what is found with older MLV002N Miyazaki test vehicle."

Air flow around front car.

COSMORAMA

ア実験線完成予想図(都留市)

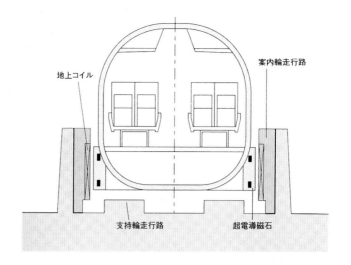

地上コイル　案内輪走行路

支持輪走行路　超電導磁石

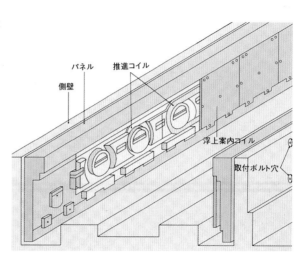

パネル　推進コイル

側壁

浮上案内コイル

取付ボルト穴

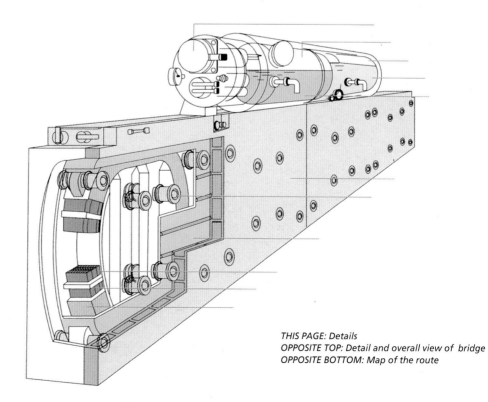

THIS PAGE: Details
OPPOSITE TOP: Detail and overall view of bridge
OPPOSITE BOTTOM: Map of the route

One of the current projects in my studio is a design proposal for an artificial island off Macau in the middle of the South China Sea, commissioned by the municipal government of Zhuhai City. We call it Haishi Jimua.

There are double implications in the term *haishi*: Its literal meaning is "city on the sea," but it also implies a mirage. Now that the municipal government is seriously considering this project and the sponsors are researching its economic and technical aspects, I cannot immediately forecast whether the *signifié* will be a city or a mirage. In any event, it is possible to see this project as utopia, because a city on the sea evokes a world totally detached from contemporary political institutions and social conventions.

It has been about half a century since we witnessed the death of many kinds of utopias, yet they are still fresh in our minds. What does it mean to project another utopia, before these others have completely disappeared?

The question of whether to consider the new utopia as a ritual of revival, a repetitive farce, or a new vision of emancipation makes our current position totally different from what preceded it. Furthermore, to realize this project involves all possible points of view. The notion of producing a project can no longer take linear relations for granted: projects no longer progress diachronically through posturing but unfold only as a negotiation among different positions.

It is interesting that Sir Thomas More –- one of the first to write about utopia – posited Nowhere Land on an island that would be discovered only after a long ocean voyage. Our artificial island will also appear in the sea, but whereas the former was envisaged in an age in which frontiers still held real expectations of new discovery, ours is placed on a sea where there is seemingly nothing left to discover. *AI*

Only East Asia still builds on a scale to rival Cecil B. de Mille. Gargantuan new cities like Shenzhen, and megatransport hubs such as Chek Lap Kok are the order of the day there. China is building bigger than all, eager to transform its economy into the biggest player on the world market. China has even dusted down that old concept, long-abandoned in the west, – utopia, and, assisted by Arata Isozaki, has given it new form.

Mirage City, or Haishi, is planned as a new island just south of Macau, which returns to mainland China next year. The Chinese Government has declared the area one of its Special Economic Development Zones and invited Isozaki to expand upon their ideas for the island to become a centre of international exchange both cultural and economic, and a focus for the whole of Asia. Isozaki plans a layout based on feng shui, with complex neighbourhood structures fusing homes and workplaces, rooted in ancient Asian urban development; and with innovative ideas such as a transport interchange where people swap dirty cars, suitable for the rest of the world, with electric vehicles designed for utopia.

Isozaki's utopia, refashioned for the post-utopian world is not a hermetically-enclosed system, but is conceived of as a "whirlpool" formed from interactions of different flows. Isozaki sees it as an alternative to today's dystopian world, in which material culture decays as the information landscape reigns. Isozaki aims to allow them to coexist and interact.

While the government is currently testing the project's viability to be constructed, Isozaki seems almost content for it to remain a mirage, in the best traditions of utopias. It is, he suggests, "in constant flux and becoming: no sooner does it convey a fixed image than it begins to counter its premise."

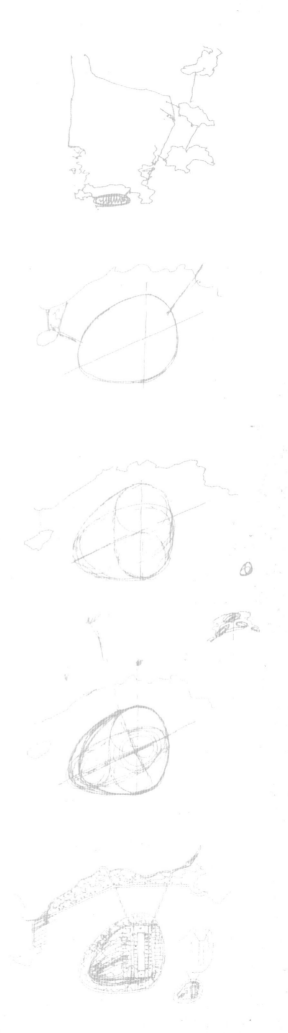

Arata Isozaki Another Utopia?

リゾート地区
Resort Area
センター地区
Central Zone
緑地
Green Zone
水上住宅地区
Water Dwellings
住宅・商業混在地区
Mixed-use
戸建住宅地区
Independent Residences
駐車場(ターミナル)地区
Parking

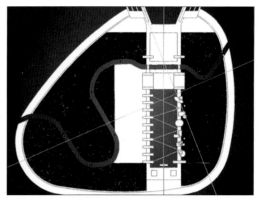

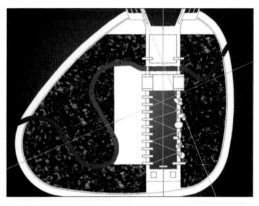

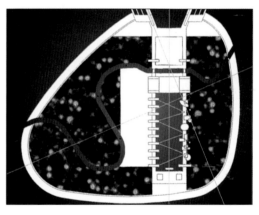

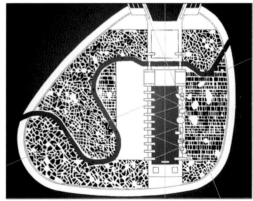

PAGE 132: Sir Thomas More's Utopia *from the 1516 edition. FAR LEFT AND PREVIOUS PAGE: Concept sketches. LEFT, MAIN PICTURE: Location map; LEFT, INSERT: Spatial placement of functions. ABOVE: Residential Formation Simulation*

Cumulative index

ARCHITECTS

Abraham, Raimund *1.13*
Ando, Tadao *1.33*, 2.58, *3.4*, *3.22* **Garden of Fine Arts, Kyoto, 3.54–9**
Asymptote *1.60*, **National Museum of Korea, Seoul, 1.84–7**
Bognar, Botond *3.5*
Bolles + Wilson *1.45*
Botta, Mario *1.52, 1.53, 1.54*
Carlo, Giancarlo de *1.48*
Cook, Peter *1.34*
Coop Himmelb(l)au *1.34, 1.51–2*, **UFA Cinema Complex, Dresden, 2.78-87**
Decq, Odile and Benoît Cornette *1.46*
Diller + Scofidio *1.47*, **Installations 2.70–7**
Domenig, Günther *1.35*
Eisenman, Peter *1.21, 1.60*, **Church of the Year 2000, Rome, Italy, 1.70–7**
Eyck, Aldo van *1.53*
Foster, Norman *1.35*
Fujii, Hiromi, **Folly in Matto City** and **Passage in the Park, 3.66–71**
Fuksas, Massimiliano *1.35*
Gehry, Frank O. *1.36*
Geipel, Finn, *1.52*
Gerkan, Meinhard von *1.36, 1.103*
Graves, Michael *1.55*
Gruhl, Hartmut *1.60*
Hadid, Zaha *1.6–7, 1.8, 1.37, 1.60*
Hara, Hiroshi, *2.60, 3.1, 3.5* **Sapporo Dome, 3.40-7**
Hasegawa, Itsuko *2.57, 3.4, 3.9*
Herzog & de Meuron *1.37*
Holl, Steven *1.38*
Irie, Kei'ichi *1.47*
Isozaki, Arata *1.38, 1.55*, **Nagi Museum of Contemporary Art, 3.86–91; Another Utopia? 3.132–5**
Ito, Toyo *1.39, 2.57, 2.62, 2.63, 3.4, 3.10* **The Odate Jukai Dome, 3.32–9**
Jumsai, Sumet *1.39*
Kleihues, Josef Paul *1.55*
Komonen, Heikkinen *1.55*
Koolhaas, Rem *1.40, 1.49, 2.3*
Krier, Léon *1.56*, **Poundbury Masterplan 2.96-105**
Kurokawa, Kisho, *3.2*, **Shenzhen SEZ, 3.92–101**
Larsen, Henning *1.56*
Libeskind, Daniel *1.61*, **V&A Museum Extension**, London, 1.78–83, *1.ifc, 1.ibc, 2.12-3*
Lund, Søren Robert *1.57*
Maki, Fumihiko *2.53*, **Makuhari Messe, 3.48–53**
Meier, Richard *1.56*
Mendini, Alessandro *1.40*
Miralles Moya, Enric *1.16, 1.41, 1.57, 1.50, 1.51*
Moneo, Rafael, *1.41*
Morphosis *1.61*, **Wagrammerstrasse Housing, Vienna 2.88-91; Sun Tower, Seoul 2.92-5**
Moss, Eric Owen *1.61*
Murcutt, Glenn *1.14*
Nouvel, Jean *1.1, 1.12, 1.42*
Papoulias, Christos *1.46*

Patkau, Patricia *1.14*
Perrault, Dominique *1.42, 1.57*
Piano, Renzo *1.15, 1.43*
Pichler, Walter *1.43*
Porphyrios, Demetri **Pitiousa, Spetses, Greece, 1.104–7**; *1.108, 1.109*
Pran, Peter *1.116, 1.117, 1.118, 1.119*
Rogers, Richard *2.1*
Rossi, Aldo *1.57*
RoTo Architects *3.11*
Sakamoto, Kazunari *2.58, 2.60*
Sejima, Kazuo *2.58*
Siza Vieira, Alvaro *1.17, 1.43, 1.57*
Smith-Miller, Henry + Laurie Hawkinson *1.47*
Sorkin, Michael *1.61*, **Urban Projects 2.106–15**
Sottsass, Ettore *1.44*
Starck, Philippe *1.44*
Suzuki, Ryoji *2.51, 3.10*
Takamatsu, Shin *3.3*, **Recent Projects 3.60-9**
Takasaki, Masaharu, **Kihoku Astronomical Museum, 3.76–9**
Tange, Kenzo *2.51*
Taniguchi, Yoshio **Toyota Municipal Museum of Art, 3.80-5**
Tschumi, Bernard **School of Architecture, Marne-la-Vallée, France, 1.62–70**
Utzon, Jørn *1.44*
Woods, Lebbeus *2.8*, **Siteline Vienna 2.64-9**
Yamamoto, Riken *2.57*, **Iwadeyama Junior High School, 3.72–5**

ARTISTS

Antoni, Janine *1.122*
Armleder, John M. *1.124*
Borofsky, Jonathan *1.124*
Clegg, Michael and Martin Guttman *1.125*
Cribber, C.G. Raving Madness and Melancholy Madness 2.122-3, *2.122, 2.123*
Duchamp, Marcel *1.125*
Gober, Robert *1.126*
Gursky, Andreas *1.120*
Holzer, Jenny *1.127*
Joannou, Dakis **Collection, 1.120-7**
Kounellis, Jannis *1.123*
McCarthy, Paul and Mike Kelley *1.126*
Nauman, Bruce **2.120-1**
Ox, Jack **From Merz to Ur, 2.116-9**
Sherman, Cindy *1.122*
Takis *1.123*

DESIGN

Contemporary Italian Silver, 2.124–5
Gehry, Frank **Furniture Design, 1.110–1**
Graves, Michael **Product Design, 1.112–5**
Maglev Trains, 3.128–31

ESSAYS

Abraham, Raimund, *Jottings*, 1.18
Ando, Tadao, *Beyond Minimalism*, 3.22
Bognar, Botond, *The Japanese Example: The Other End of Architecture*, 2.49
Japanese Architecture: Towards the twenty-first Century (Report from the Site), 3.8
Coop Himmelb(l)au, *The Architecture of Clouds*, 2.15
Eimert, Dorothea, *Paper, Chance and Deconstructivism*, 1.58
Eisenman, Peter, *Presentness and the "Being-Only-Once" of Architecture*, 1.20
Fatouros, Dimitri, *The End of Place?*, 2.14
Frampton, Kenneth, *Technology, Place and Architecture*, 1.12
Fukuyama, Francis, *The End of Order*, 2.20
Gerkan, Meinhard von, *Renaissance of Railway Stations – Nuclei of a New Stage in Urban Development*, 1.102
Hollein, Hans, *Sensing the Future: The Architect as Seismograph*, 1.30
Horgan, John, *The End of Chaoplexity*, 2.16
Ito, Toyo, *Three Transparencies*, 3.12
Krier, L., *Prospects for a New Urbanism*, 1.96
Kurokawa, Kisho, *Abstract Geometry and Contemporary Architecture*, 1.28, *The Eco-Media City in the Age of Symbiosis*, 3.18
Libeskind, Daniel, *Traces of the Unborn*, 2.12
Melhuish, C., *Reaching for the Future*, 1.8
Moss, Eric Owen, *The Glue*, 2.24
Nitschke, Günther, *Chinju no mori – Urban Deity Groves*, 3.24
Papadakis, Andreas, *Future Uncertain*, 1.6; *The End of Innovation*, 2.6
Schulz, Evelyn, *A Confucian Critique of Modern Tokyo and its Future: Koda Rohan's* One Nation's Capital, 3.28
Takasaki, Masaharu, *Kagoshima Cosmology*, 3.16
Tschumi, Bernard, *Architecture/Events*, 1.24
Woods, Lebbeus, *The Crisis of Innovation*, 2.20

LANDSCAPE DESIGN

Walker, Johnson & Partners 1.3, 1.17, **Three Minimalist Gardens 1.88–95**
Watanabe, Makoto-Sei *3.4–5*, **The Fibre Wave at K Museum, 3.102–7**

TECHNOLOGY

Nikken Sekkei Ltd, **Osaka Dome, 3.108–21**
Takenaka Corporation, **Odate Jukai Dome, 3.32–9**

THE SCHOOLS

The Architectural Association 2.126-41
The LA Experience 1.132–43
SCI-Arc 1.133, 1.135
UCLA 1.140, 1.141
USC 1.136, 1.137
Woodbury 1.143
Japan 3.122–7
Shibauru Institute of Technology 3.124
Tokyo Institute of Technology 3.122
University of Tokyo 3.126

The prefix indicates the number of the issue:

1 - NA1 REACHING FOR THE FUTURE
2 - NA2 THE END OF INNOVATION
3 - NA3 JAPAN AT THE CUTTING EDGE

Extensive presentation is indicated in bold.

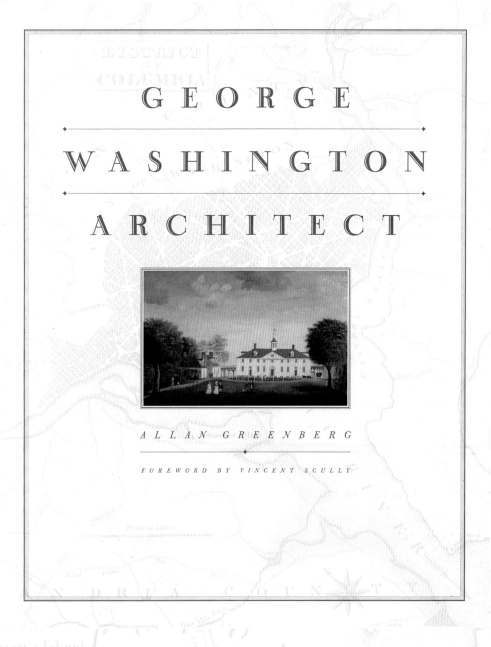

GEORGE

WASHINGTON

ARCHITECT

ALLAN GREENBERG

FOREWORD BY VINCENT SCULLY

George Washington, Architect
by Allan Greenberg
with Foreword by Vincent Scully

9 1/2 x 12in (300 x 240mm)
170 pages
colour photos, line drawings
Hardback
$55.00/£35.00
isbn 1 901092 18 6
Publication: May

Soldier, statesman, gentleman farmer, nation builder. More than two centuries after George Washington retired from office and quietly returned to his Virginia estate, his accomplishments continue to evoke an outpouring of biographies, chronicles, and critiques. But one talent has been overlooked. In George Washington, Architect, Allan Greenberg explores the first president's innovations as a designer of buildings and landscapes. Quoting from primary documents, including Washington's correspondence and journals, Greenberg reveals that Washington was an exemplary form-giver whose best work was conducted in his own backyards: Mount Vernon and Washington D.C.

The first part of this volume reveals how Washington not only redesigned the exterior and interior of Mount Vernon, but also sculpted the terrain, rearranged vistas, designed farm buildings and created one of the most beautiful American gardens. The second part concerns the new capital of the United States itself which symbolically expresses the principles of the first democratic republic in history

As an architect inspired by Washington, Allan Greenberg has himself contributed distinguished buildings to the United States for the past three decades. In *George Washington, Architect*, he explores the construction of a nation, a city, a house, and a farm as a unified activity directed by a single – and singular – genius.

PORPHYRIOS
ASSOCIATES

Demetri Porphyrios's buildings and urban design are characterized by an unerring instinct for appropriate materials – generally indigenous and natural – harmonious proportions and contextual sensitivity.Many have spoken of the connection between tectonics and form but almost no one has put this into practice with the richness and maturity of Porphyrios. His architecture is not about style; it is about living traditions open to adaptation and responsive to region, climate, nature and culture.

The work presented here, all completed within the past five years, from urban projects to office, institutional and college buildings, includes office buildings in Birmingham, the New Courts, Theatre and Library at Selwyn College, Cambridge, a new quadrangle at Magdalen College, Oxford, the town of Pitiousa in Spetses, selected residential buildings, and a number of urban projects for resort towns and inner city developments throughout the world.

Introductions by the historian and architect Professor Paolo Portoghesi and by Dr. Oswyn Murray, Fellow of Balliol College, Oxford, examine the work. "The work of Porphyrios," writes Paolo Portoghesi, "has the quality of creativity which finds itself not in academic repetitions but in the classical as a way of life. His work has a spontaneity and a capacity to adapt itself to a place, and of expressing the harmony between man and nature."

Porphyrios Associates
Recent Works
Essays by Paolo Portoghesi,
Oswyn Murray and Demetri
Porphyrios
Series: NA MONOGRAPHS

9 1/2 x 12in (300 x 240mm)
208 pages
Fully illustrated, mostly in colour

Paperback $45.00/£27.50
isbn 1-901092-13-5

Hardback $55.00/£35.00
isbn 1-901092-14-3

Publication: April

NA MONOGRAPH

PETER PRAN

JONATHAN WARD TIMOTHY JOHNSON PAUL DAVIS
essays
CHRISTIAN NORBERG-SCHULZ
KENNETH FRAMPTON
FUMIHIKO MAKI
JUHANI PALLASMAA

an architecture of poetic movement

altered perceptions

ANDREAS PAPADAKIS PUBLISHER

Peter Pran
An Architecture of Poetic Movement
Essays by Kenneth Frampton,
Christian Norberg-Schulz,
Fumihiko Maki, Juhani Pallasmaa
Series: NA MONOGRAPHS

9 1/2 x 12in (300 x 240mm)
144 pages
Fully illustrated, mostly in colour

Paperback $45.00/£27.50
isbn 1-901092-13-5

Hardback $55.00/£35.00
isbn 1-901092-14-3

Available now

An introduction to the philosophy and design methods of Peter Pran and his team, now based at NBBJ in Seattle. Pran is the winner of many competitions, honours and commissions worldwide, and is noted for the professionalism and technological skill of his designs and computer-modelling techniques.

Over the years, he has won twenty honorary awards from The American Institute of Architects and twelve international competitions, including the New York State Psychiatric Institute and the New York City Policy Academy and, most recently, the Seoul Dome for the 2002 World Cup and Telenor Headquarters in Oslo, Norway.

Peter Pran has always worked on his cutting-edge designs with a team of young designers using state-of-the-art computer technology. Rather than importing the computer into traditional design he has completely rethought the whole process enabling him to work in three dimensions and to provide his prospective clients with a clear vision of their future building both inside and out and its impact on the site. With its introduction by Christian Norberg-Schulz, essays by Kenneth Frampton, Fumihiko Maki, and Juhani Pallasma, the detailed presentation of all recent work, and appendices that include a list of selected buildings and projects and an annotated bibliograpy, this NA Monograph provides an essential introduction to the work of this important international architect.

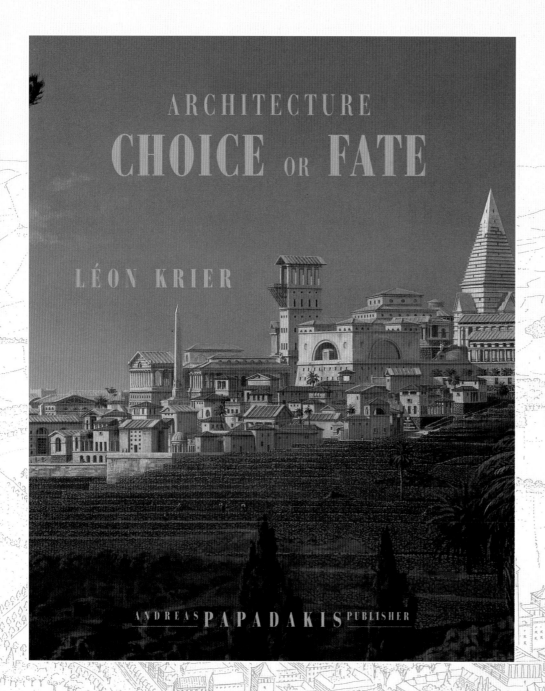

ARCHITECTURE
CHOICE OR FATE

LÉON KRIER

ANDREAS PAPADAKIS PUBLISHER

Léon Krier, theorist and reformer of modern traditional architecture and urbanism, reveals in this layman's manifesto why, in matters of democracy, architecture is far behind politics. Living in a traditional home and driving a fast car are not incompatible as modernists would have us believe. We are in fact witnessing a worldwide renaissance of traditional architecture and urbanism and its near universal condemnation by the modernist mafia has had no influence on rising sales of traditional houses. We live in society of free choice in politics and food, in religion and lifestyle, in work and jobs. And so why should our choice be restricted in architecture and urbanism?

The fact that modernism has never been a popular choice is not, according to Krier, due to people's ignorance but to modernism's own conceptual poverty. Architecture cannot be left to architects alone. We all have to live with architecture and we all have strong feelings about it, whether knowingly or unconsciously, simply because we like or dislike a place, a house, a city.

This polemic is essential reading for anyone concerned with the state and direction of architecture and urban planning today. It will provoke wide-ranging discussion and will be a vital tool in the renaissance of the art of building cities that are pleasant and agreeable to live in, an art we are in danger of losing.

Architecture – Choice or Fate
by Léon Krier

9 1/2 x 12in (300 x 240mm)
220pp, including 12 in colour,
line drawings by the author

Paperback with flaps
$39.00 / £24.95
isbn 1 901092 03 8

Available now

Winner of the Silver Medal of the Académie française

THE TRUE, THE FICTIVE, AND THE REAL

THE HISTORICAL DICTIONARY OF ARCHITECTURE

OF

QUATREMÈRE DE QUINCY

INTRODUCTORY ESSAYS AND SELECTED TRANSLATIONS
BY
SAMIR YOUNÉS

ANDREAS PAPADAKIS PUBLISHER

The True, the Fictive and the Real
Quatremère de Quincy's
Historical Dictionary of
Architecture
Essays and translations by
Samir Younés

9 1/2 x 12in (300 x 240mm)
256 pages
84 b&w illustrations

Hardback
$55.00/£35.00
isbn 1 901092 17 8

Publication: May

"This is not merely a repertory of ancient words and sounds; it is a living inventory of all those concepts and ideas without which there can be no true architecture as art or craft." Léon Krier

"This is a seminal analysis of the ideas of Quatremère de Quincy and of the profound implications they have for contemporary architectural theory." Demetri Porphyrios

Antoine Chrysostôme Quatremère de Quincy (1755-1849) was one of the most influential French art and architectural theorists. His career included programmes to reform the Académie, the transformation of the church of Sainte-Geneviève into the French Pantheon, his magisterial contribution to the *Encyclopédie Méthodique* of C.J. Panckoucke (1788-1825), and his unprecedented hegemony over l'Ecole des Beaux-Arts from 1816 until 1839.

This volume provides the first English translation of the theoretical essays from his seminal work, *Le Dictionnaire Historique d'Architecture* of 1832. The importance of this *Dictionnaire* stems from Quatremère's profound reflections on the nature and the ends of architecture; on the principles which are at the source of her rules, and on the roles of imitation and invention within tradition.

RECENT TITLES

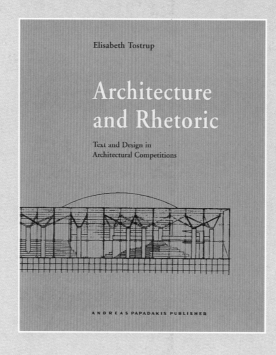

Architecture and Rhetoric
Text and Design in Architectural Competitions, Oslo 1939-1997
by Elisabeth Tostrup

9 1/2 x 12in (300 x 240mm)
208pages, copiously illustrated in b&w
Hardback
$55/£35
isbn 1 901092 05 4
Publication: April

All architecture is, in a sense, rhetoric in that the architect attempts to persuade, to put across a way of seeing or living in space. Of course he does this with the building itself but first the decision has to be taken to build it. In this volume Professor Tostrup discusses how architecture gets built via the architectural competition, perhaps the most prominent and symbolic way in which society chooses the built form of the future. Architectural competitions are, fundamentally, a debate in which the architect, uses drawings, models and text to convince both the jury and the public of the potential for the future offered by his vision.

Classical Architecture
by Demetri Porphyrios

9 3/4 x 12in (300 x 248mm)
156 pages, over 200 illus., mostly colour
Paperback with flaps
$35.00/£19.50
isbn 1 901092 06 2
Available now

This perceptive book is an exploration of architecture as the art of building tracing it back to its roots in Ancient Greece and Rome. It is now available for the first time in a quality paperback at an accessible price. This is both a pedagogic and a critical book that has implications for present-day theory of style, our view of history, and for the practice of architecture. Demetri Porphyrios, an important international architect, celebrates the richness of traditional forms and techniques, and, in our age of pluralism, argues for the relevance of a historically informed architecture that "continually searches for and brings out the new."

Restructuring the City
Two international urban design competitions for Thessaloniki
by Vilma Hastaoglou

9 1/2 x 12in (300 x 240mm)
248 pages, including 152 in colour
Paperback with flaps
$48/£30
isbn 1 901092 16 X
Available now

The prizewinning entries in the competitions for redesigning Thessaloniki's two most prominent urban landscapes – the waterfront and the civic axis – make an important contribution to a solution of the age-old problem of creating in existing landscapes adventurous architecture that respects the memory and identity of ancient sites. The aim was to refocus the entire city, drawing on its tumultuous past to build a future role for Greece's second city as a crossroads of Balkan culture and commerce. Projects by Toyo Ito; Manuel de Solà Morales; Vittorio Gregotti; Eleni Gigantes, Elias Zenghelis, Panos Koulermos; and Doxiadis Associates.

NEW ARCHITECTURE is an exciting new international series on contemporary thought and practice in architecture and urban design.

NEW ARCHITECTURE presents the work and writing not only of all the top international architects and theorists, but also of the young and innovative who have not yet made their mark. It carries up-to-date information and critical comment on what is happening now in the worlds of Architectural Theory and Design, Urbanism, Design, Technology, Landscape and the Fine Arts. It has features on significant competitions, exhibitions, conferences and books and devotes a special section to design and theoretical work coming out of the world's best schools of architecture.

NEW ARCHITECTURE looks critically at current directions, irrespective of stylistic and theoretical considerations, and explores each issue in depth, raising all the most important questions posed by the developing role of architecture in the world today.

Editorial Board: Tadao Ando, Mario Botta, Peter Eisenman, Dimitri Fatouros, Kenneth Frampton, Meinhard von Gerkan, Jorge Glusberg, Michael Graves, Allan Greenberg, Hans Hollein, Josef Paul Kleihues, Panos Koulermos, Léon Krier, Kisho Kurokawa, Henning Larsen, Daniel Libeskind, Richard Meier, Enric Miralles, Jean Nouvel, Cesar Pelli, Demetri Porphyrios, Paolo Portoghesi, Peter Pran, Hani Rashid, Jacquelin Robertson, Alvaro Siza, Robert A.M. Stern, Bernard Tschumi

Subscriptions are available for six consecutive numbers at $130/£90 (student rate $90/£60) from the London office only.

Booksellers may wish to place a standing order for this series. Individual volumes are supplied at the usual trade terms.

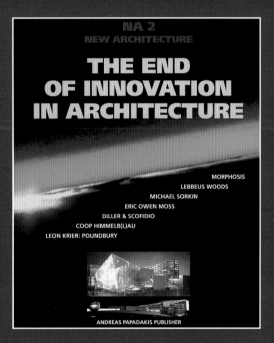

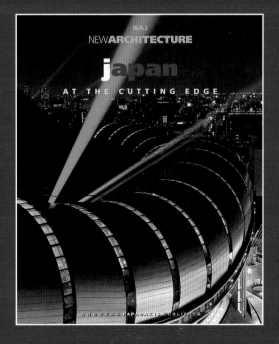

This first number takes its theme from Hans Hollein's exhibition *The Architect as Seismograph*; Kenneth Frampton's seminar on *Technology, Place and Architecture*; the work of Peter Eisenman, Daniel Libeskind and Bernard Tschumi; the Los Angeles Schools; and a polemic book by Léon Krier, with sections on urban design, landscape, product design and art.

NA1 – Reaching for the Future

9 1/2 x 12in (300 x 240mm)
144 pages, over 150 illustrations
Paperback with flaps $27.50/£17.50
isbn 1 901092 01 1
Available now

When Daedalos murdered Talos it was to protect his position as the most innovative architect of his age. Three millennia later we examine the obsession of the architect with innovation and the new. Architects featured include Lebbeus Woods, Daniel Libeskind, Coop Himmelb(l)au, Eric Owen Moss, Michael Sorkin Studio. Articles by John Horgan and Francis Fukyama.

NA2 – The End of Innovation
9 1/2 x 12in (300 x 240mm)
144 pages, over 150 illustrations
Paperback with flaps $27.50/£17.50
isbn 1 901092 01 1
Available now

Responding boldly, but often critically, to the rapid encroachments of the information age, Japanese architects are shaping the architecture of the future with all its promises, doubts and contradictions. Featured architects include Ando, Hara, Isozaki, Ito, Kurokawa, Maki, Takamatsu, Takasaki, Taniguchi, Watanabe, Yamamoto. Edited by Boton Bognar.

NA3 – Japan at the Cutting Edge
9 1/2 x 12in (300 x 240mm)
144 pages, over 150 illustrations
Paperback with flaps $27.50/£17.50
isbn 1 901092 01 1
Available now

ORDER FORM

I would like to order the following books:

____	Arwas	THE ART OF GLASS	hb 1 901092 00 3	$35.00 / £17.50
____	Greenberg	GEORGE WASHINGTON, ARCH	hb 1 901092 18 6	$65.00 / £35.00
____	Hastaoglou	RESTRUCTURING THE CITY	pb 1 901092 16 X	$48.00 / £30.00
____	Krier, L.	ARCHITECTURE: CHOICE OR FATE	pb 1 901092 03 8	$39.00 / £24.95
____	Loew	PROMOTION OF ARCHITECTURE	pb 1 901092 02 X	$12.00 / £ 7.95
____	Porphyrios	CLASSICAL ARCHITECTURE	pb 1 901092 06 2	$35.00 / £19.50
____	Tostrup	ARCHITECTURE AND RHETORIC	hb 1 901092 05 4	$55.00 / £35.00
____	Younés	QUATREMERE DE QUINCY	hb 1 901092 17 8	$55.00 / £35.00

NEW ARCHITECTURE

____	NA 1	REACHING FOR THE FUTURE	pb 1 901092 01 1	$27.50 / £17.50
____	NA 2	THE END OF INNOVATION	pb 1 901092 09 7	$27.50 / £17.50
____	NA 3	JAPAN AT THE CUTTING EDGE	pb 1 901092 10 0	$27.50 / £17.50

NA MONOGRAPHS

____	NAM1	PETER PRAN.	pb 1 901092 07 0	$37.50 / £22.50
			hb 1 901092 08 9	$45.00 / £27.50
____	NAM2	PORPHYRIOS ASSOCIATES	pb 1 901092 13 5	$45.00 / £27.50
			hb 1 901092 14 3	$55.00 / £35.00

Payment enclosed by Cheque / Money Order / Draft $.....................
£.....................

Please charge £ .... to my credit card
Account No. ....
Expiry date ....

Name ....

Address ....
..
..
Signature ....

ANDREAS PAPADAKIS PUBLISHER
107 Park Street, London W1Y 3FB
Tel. 0171 499 0444 Fax 0171 499 0222

144 *New Books*

NEW ARCHITECTURE SUBSCRIPTION FORM

Payment enclosed by Cheque / Money Order / Draft $...............
£...............

Please charge £ .... to my credit card
Account No. ....
Expiry date ....

Name ....

Address ....
....
Signature ....

NEW ARCHITECTURE subscription rates

6 consecutive issues	$135	£90
Student rate	$ 90	£60

Students in full time education please attach
photocopy of studencard
Rates subject to change without notice
Payments other than £sterling or US dollars
please add £6 or $10 to cover currency charges

Individual numbers of NEW ARCHITECTURE are available at
$27.50 / £17.50 plus $5 or £2.50 for postage and packing

I wish to subscribe to NEW ARCHITECTURE
at the full rate ...... at the student rate ......